discus

gunter keller

Cover: Turquoise discus. Photo by Hans J. Mayland.

Frontispiece: Brown discus. Photo by Jiri Taborsky.

All line drawings, unless otherwise indicated, are by Hermann Kacher, Hans Herman Kropf, and Peter Lohle.

ISBN 0-87666-457-5

Originally published by Franckh'sche Verlagshandlung, W. Keller & Co., Stuttgart/1974 under the title *Der Diskus, König der Aquarienfische.*

First edition ©1974 by Franckh'sche Verlagshandlung.

Distributed in the U.S.A. by T.F.H. Publications, Inc., 211 West Sylvania Avenue, P.O. Box 27, Neptune City, N.J. 07753; in England by T.F.H. (Gt. Britain) Ltd., 13 Nutley Lane, Reigate, Surrey; in Canada to the book store and library trade by Clarke, Irwin & Company, Clarwin House, 791 St. Clair Avenue West, Toronto 10, Ontario; in Canada to the pet trade by Rolf C. Hagen Ltd., 3225 Sartelon Street, Montreal 382, Quebec; in Southeast Asia by Y.W. Ong, 9 Lorong 36 Geylang, Singapore 14; in Australia and the south Pacific by Pet Imports Pty. Ltd., P.O. Box 149, Brookvale 2100, N.S.W., Australia. Published by T.F.H. Publications, Inc. Ltd., The British Crown Colony of Hong Kong.

CONTENTS

This "turquoise discus" developed in Germany looks just as beautiful as the original turquoise discus developed by Jack Wattley in the United States. Photo by Hans J. Mayland.

Shown is a natural "red discus" from Brazil. This variety is not too common in nature. The bright red coloration of some discus fishes from the Far East is artificially induced. Photo by Hans J. Mayland.

A pair of *Symphysodon aequifasciata* worthy of being the subject of a prize-winning photo by Dudley Campbell.

WHAT ARE DISCUS FISHES?

Discus fishes have fascinated aquarists and ichthyologists from the time of their introduction into the tropical fish hobby and are the pride of many freshwater aquarists today. They have also posed many problems to their keepers; luckily, solutions to most of those problems have now been found. In addition, discus-keeping has led to new developments in the hobby, and those developments affect the tropical fish field in general in a good way—even people who don't keep discus have benefited from them.

Ichthyologists today are still engaged in the task of clarifying the morphology, ecology, and systematics of the discus fishes. Over the past fifteen years many discoveries have helped to make the keeping of discus fishes *almost* problem-free. To inform you about the problems—and their solutions—is the aim of this book.

Discus fishes owe their name to their shape, resembling as it does a discus in a vertical position. In the zoological system the discus fish belongs to the order Perciformes (perch-shaped fishes), sub-order Percoidea (perch·like fishes), family Cichlidae. This family encompasses many species in many genera, among them the genus *Symphysodon* (**symphysis** = joint of the two branches of the lower jaw, **odus** = tooth) which contains nothing but discus fishes. So far, so good—but now come the uncertainties. There is a lot of confusion about the number of species of discus fishes. Some say there is only one species, and some say there are at least two. The ones who say there is only one species base their conclusion on the fact that discus fishes of all types, regardless of color and other superficial differences, interbreed and produce offspring that are 100% fertile themselves. Additionally, they all live in the wild in the same place. The ones who say that there are at least two species base their belief on the fact that ichthyologists have described at least two different species, and separating the two species are (according to the ichthyologists) differences other than color alone.

A *Symphysodon discus* caught in the Rio Negro near Manaus, Brazil, and photographed by Harald Schultz. The fins apparently were slightly damaged during its capture.

Opposite:
The median, ocular, and caudal peduncle bands are discernible, but the narrower intervening bands in this *Symphysodon discus* are not. The longitudinal light blue bands are particularly distinct in this individual. Photo by Wolfgang Bechtle.

This picture of a breeding pair of *Symphysodon discus* shows dramatically that the color pattern is under voluntary control of individual fish. Photo by Muller Schmida.

The systematic division according to Schultz 1960 which at present is still being upheld subdivides the genus *Symphysodon* into two species:

1. *Symphysodon discus* Heckel 1840 (true discus)
2. *Symphysodon aequifasciata*, comprised of the subspecies
   Symphysodon aequifasciata axelrodi Schultz 1960 (brown discus)
   Symphysodon aequifasciata aequifasciata Pellegrin 1903 (green discus)
   Symphysodon aequifasciata haraldi Schultz 1960 (blue discus)

The color varieties are known to most discus fanciers by their popular names and generally are available on the market. But there are other color varieties besides, offered for sale under the names "royal-blue discus," "turquoise discus," "red discus," "four-color discus," and "pompadour discus," to name just a few. The names for some of these color varieties are mere trade names. The differences in color among them, as compared to the differences in color of the subspecies listed above, are so minimal that there is little to support their classification as separate races, particularly since some of the varieties mentioned are hybrids. It is too early, therefore, to be sure about the exact nomenclature. One has to wait and see and leave it to the ichthyologists to make the final decision. However, to enable the aquarists to identify their discus fishes I shall now give a description of the animals according to their color. Dr. Hermann Meinken has already done this in detail, and the following is based on his work, apart from a few deviations.

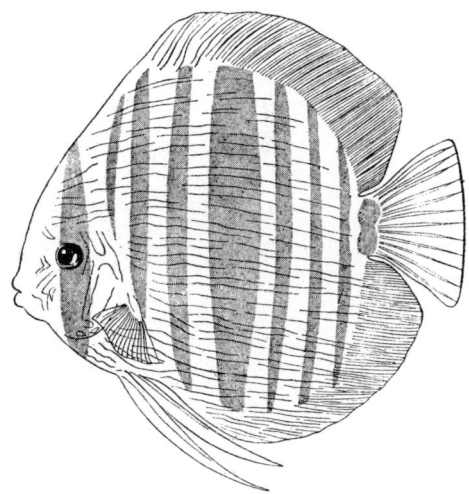

True discus (*Symphysodon discus*).

Symphysodon discus Heckel 1840

Basic color of the body more or less light brown or gray-brown, covered down the whole length of the body by about 15-18 pale blue to white-blue longitudinal bands which are irregular and slightly wavy. These longitudinal bands can, however, also be confined to the dorsal and abdominal region. They start on the forehead and behind the operculum and terminate at the base of the caudal fin. The dorsal and anal fins lie within their range. In addition, these fins have a 7-10 mm broad black border which also goes through the base of the caudal fin. This black band is covered with blue longitudinal lines and rows of speckles going in the direction of the fin rays. The outer rim of the dorsal and anal fins may be more or less red in color. The protracted ventral fins are red and covered with one or more blue longitudinal bands. The tips are yellowish red. The cheeks are

11

When frightened, for example by a strong light used in taking photographs, a fish like this brown discus can temporarily lose its body pattern. Photo by Jiri Taborsky.

Opposite:
A pair of young adult brown discus (*Symphysodon aequifasciata axelrodi*). Note the absence of an unusually wide body band. Photo by Miloslav Kocar.

adorned with shiny blue irregular patches or short bands. Vertically across the body run nine brown-black bands of varying intensity and breadth. The first band extends from the neck across the eye and almost down to the base of the ventral fin. Bands II to IV are very faint and not always visible. The fifth band starts where the soft part of the dorsal fin begins, traverses the middle of the body and, as a rule, terminates at the onset of the soft anal fin. This brown-black or black band is broader and more intense in color than the others. Stripes VI to VIII are again very faint and barely visible. In contrast, the black stripe at the base of the caudal fin is very prominent. This characteristic of the three stripes—especially of the broad stripe in the middle —is diagnostic of *Symphysodon discus* Heckel. The color of the eyes varies in these animals. Usually the eyes are red, with a golden ring around the pupil. But very often one also comes across fish with amber-colored and brownish eyes.

The prominent pattern of cross bands is one of the specific characteristics of this fish. These stripes are formed by pigment cells which react to certain stimuli by expanding or contracting. Irritation can have a number of different causes; it is usually transmitted via the central nervous system. In all discus varieties, the changing of the cross-band pattern reflects certain conditions of excitement and behavior. Particularly in situations where fear is experienced or one fish has to submit to the dominance of another, fish of a uniform dark-brown color can change into light buff-colored individuals with strong black stripes. This can frequently be seen in photographs, when all varieties show eight to nine cross bands. Eight run across the body and one forms part of the black border of the dorsal and anal fin above the caudal peduncle. This latter stripe seems much less influenced by the conduction of stimuli than do the others—in all varieties it is almost always visible.

The other bands, however, are very much affected; they show every degree of intensity and at times may also become totally invisible. Nor are all bands at all times necessarily subject to the same stimuli; at any time some bands may be more or less prominent than others.

Symphysodon discus Heckel also shows these variations. But its fifth band, the median stripe, is *always* broader and stronger than the other bands. In other discus varieties this is not the case. This discus is not called the "true discus" because it is more genuine than its cousins but because the first description of the genus *Symphysodon*, which was carried out in 1840, was based on it. Discus specimens subsequently caught (presumably the brown discus) do not quite fit the description. Later, when new specimens of *Symphysodon discus* Heckel had been found and matched the original description, one had re-discovered the "real" or "true" discus, and so it has remained until today.

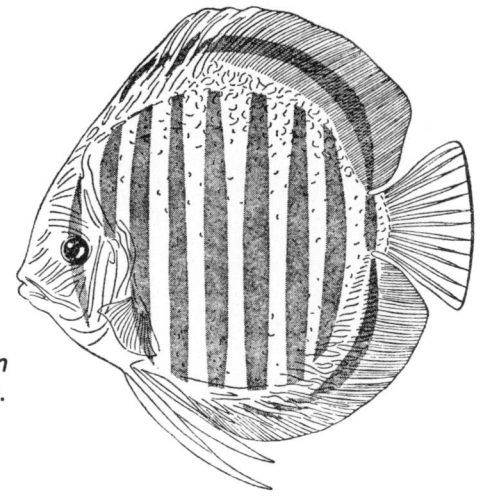

Green discus (*Symphysodon aequifasciata aequifasciata*).

Symphysodon aequifasciata aequifasciata Pellegrin 1903 (Green Discus)

The basic color of this fish again is a very variable brown; it ranges from yellowish buff to olive-brown. The blue-green longitudinal lines usually run only from the forehead over the dorsal region and continue into the dorsal fin. The ventral side is frequently covered with only a few lines, its main characteristic being an expanse of green which incorporates the whole anal fin. The green is interrupted by red stripes or speckles which can sometimes be found all over the body. Again the dorsal and anal fin are enclosed by a black band which extends to the caudal peduncle and covers it like a bandage. This band is bordered and adorned with blue-green stripes and spots; the outer rim of the fins is sometimes bright red in color. The ventral fins also are red and covered with blue-green stripes. Head and cheeks are covered with lines of the same color.

In these fish, too, the color of the eyes varies from red to yellow. Characteristic are the eight to nine vertical cross bands which in this case are of the same breadth and occasionally of the same intensity as well. The green coloration is very variable in these fish. Here, too, one can sometimes see completely striated animals with many red lines, and sometime soon, no doubt, someone is going to create the "royal green discus" from such individuals.

A close-up of a green discus (*S. aequifasciata aequifasciata*) whose nine body bars are very well marked. Photo by Dr. Eduard Schmidt-Focke.

Opposite:
A semi-frontal view of the head of a brown discus shows the arrangement of the blue lines on the forehead. Photo by Arend van den Nieuwenhuizen.

Symphysodon aequifasciata axelrodi Schultz 1960 (Brown Discus)

Body predominantly brown to gray-brown. Only a few blue longitudinal stripes on forehead and neck. Dorsal and anal fin with blue lines and speckles. The outer rim of these fins is pale red. The vertical fins are red, too, and covered with blue striations. Again we find those nine black vertical bands on the body.

The eyes are red to brown-black. This discus fish, the one most frequently kept in the aquarium, has been named in honor of Dr. Herbert R. Axelrod.

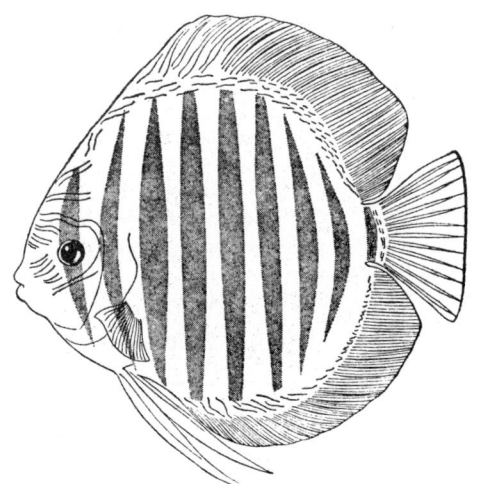

Brown discus (*Symphysodon aequifasciata axelrodi*).

Symphysodon aequifasciata haraldi Schultz 1960 (Blue Discus)

As in the above-mentioned variety, the basic color is brown to gray-brown. But, as opposed to the brown discus, the strong blue longitudinal lines extend from the head over the back into the dorsal fin. The anal fin shows a lot of red, and so does the outer rim of the dorsal fin. In its other characteristics the blue discus resembles the brown discus.

Color variety "Royal Blue"

Identical with *S. aequifasciata haraldi*. This name is reserved only for individuals with a particularly powerful blue coloration in which the blue longitudinal lines also run along the middle of the body, making the fish appear completely striated. Dorsal and anal

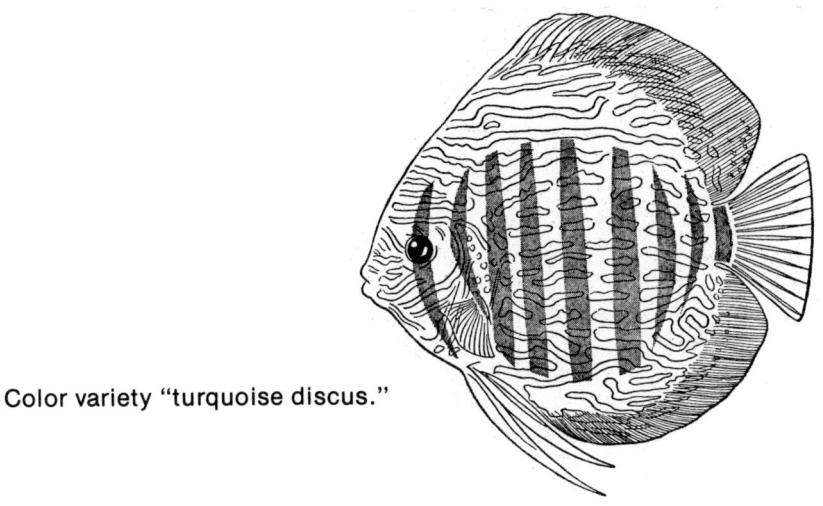

Color variety "turquoise discus."

fins are closely covered with blue lines. The nine cross bands are as obvious as they are in the varieties mentioned above. Other characteristics as per *S.a. haraldi*. This variety is invariably caught along with *S.a. haraldi* and *S.a. axelrodi*. It is found mostly in the Rio Purus region. Here the animals are distinguished by longitudinal lines which are very broad and straight. Undoubtedly they are among the most attractive of discus fishes. This variety was given its name by Willi Schwartz, an exporter in Manaus, Brazil.

These very colorful animals are caught and imported only in limited numbers, which means they are considered highly desirable and are greatly sought after.

Color variety "Turquoise Discus"

Basic color similar to that of the color varieties described earlier, though often a slightly lighter brown. The pure blue in this case is replaced by a shiny blue-green or white-green. The longitudinal striations are less broad and straight, as in the "royal blue," and more wavy and interrupted. The dorsal fin and the anal fin especially contain numerous red striations. The ventral fin is distinguished by an equally intense red. Color of the eyes predominantly red. This fish is another one that occasionally shows its nine cross bands as being of identical intensity and breadth. Jack Wattley, an American fish breeder, first introduced this color variety (in 1969) under this name. The specimens concerned were fish bred in captivity. This variety is another one of great beauty.

A blue discus taken from its natural habitat in Brazil. Note the extent of the blue lines on the dorsal fin and the wider brown horizontal stripes on this fish. Photo by Dr. Herbert R. Axelrod.

Opposite:
Specimens of blue discus recently collected by Dr. Herbert R. Axelrod in Tefe, Brazil. He reports that each river system has its own characteristic color variation. A closer examination shows slight variations in the color pattern. Photo by Dr. Herbert R. Axelrod.

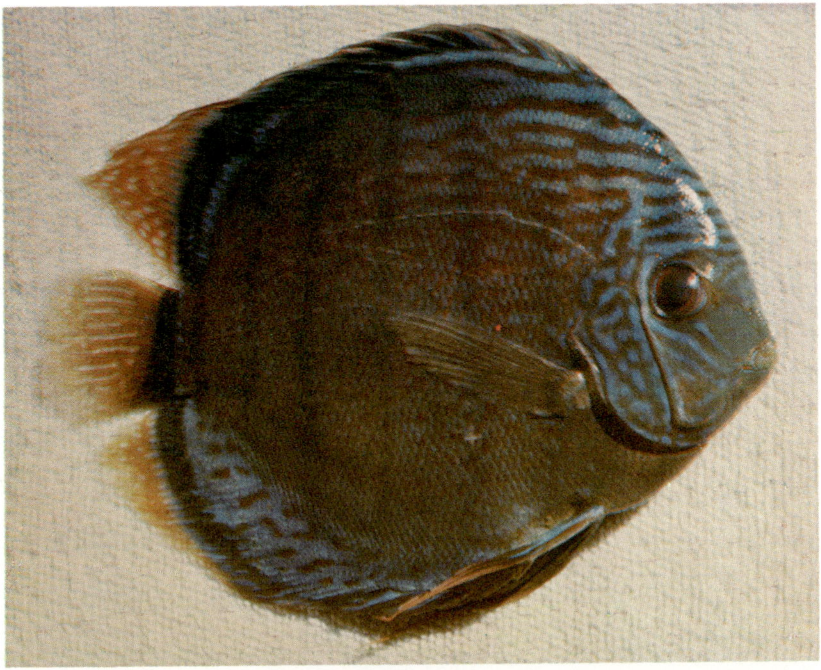

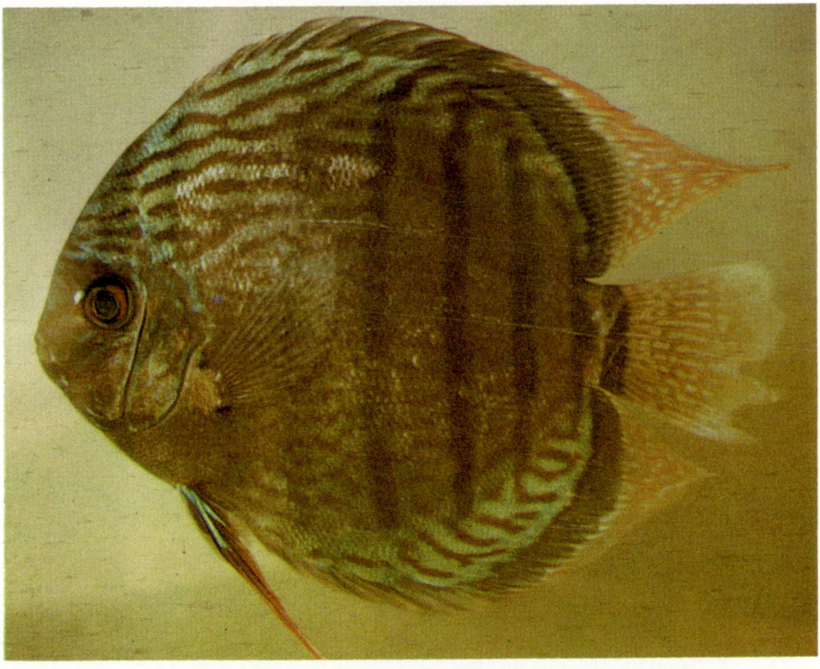

Color variety "Pompadour Discus"

In Great Britain, the United States, and Canada this is the name given by some to *Symphysodon discus* Heckel. Since it is applied to all sorts of color varieties, the name is too vague to be of much use.

Color variety "Red Discus"

Basic color yellowish brown to red-brown. Only a few blue longitudinal lines covering the back and the anal and dorsal fins. These fins are strikingly red; some areas of the body are covered with red or brown-red spots. Especially the margins of the anal and dorsal fin and the ventral fins are of an intense red. The nine cross bands and the black border of the anal and dorsal fins resemble those in the other color varieties. The "red discus" most certainly is a variation of the "brown discus." Imports are more red-brown in color, but this is greatly dependent on the colors of water and light. The red color is probably caused by dietary substances. The progeny of red discus fish bred in Germany no longer show the striking coloration seen in imported animals. In tropical fish stores one sometimes comes across very red fish which have been bred in captivity in Southeast Asia, but in this case certain dyes in the food are largely responsible for the color.

A holding trap for discus and other tropical fish constructed by professional collectors in the backwaters of the Rio Negro. As many as 50,000 small tropical fishes and a few hundred discus can be held in the trap pictured. Photo by Dr. Herbert R. Axelrod.

These are newly caught discus in the holding tank of a commercial dealer in Manaus. The normal color pattern is faded on account of the shock of being handled. It will eventually return when the fish have adjusted to the new container. Photo by Dr. Herbert R. Axelrod.

As we can see, the genus *Symphysodon* is a richly colorful one. Undoubtedly we can expect the emerging of yet another color variety or two which will be endowed with very promising names. At present, for example, a cobalt-blue discus is being much advertised. It should, however, not become the fashion of the day that every breeder sells his mixed products under some fanciful name.

Apart from the deviations in color, the individual varieties also show differences in the structure of their bodies and fins. In certain areas, for instance, occur very high-finned forms in which the body appears smaller than it actually is. In *Symphysodon discus* Heckel this can be observed quite frequently. Other variations have a smaller and very round dorsal fin. The black band bordering the dorsal and anal fins can also differ in breadth and intensity in some variations. Even today it is no longer easy to distinguish the varieties that occur in nature, but it may become altogether impossible when the differences have been blotted out by indiscriminate hybridization of the fish that were bred in captivity. Then one will no longer be able to provide reliable information about the fish that swim in hobbyists' tanks. There is no doubt that more and more people are opting for the "more beautiful" varieties, i.e., the most colorful animals. But nature has shown herself to be thrifty here—so far, only limited numbers of these varieties have been caught. To propagate these fishes and make them more widely available would be a rewarding task for responsible breeders.

An aquarium-bred red discus. In this particular photograph the body bands are not evident. This condition is, however, only temporary. Photo by Gunter Keller.

This hybrid resulted from a cross between a red discus caught in Brazil near Peru and a turquoise green-striped discus. The hybridization was accomplished by Dr. Eduard Schmidt-Focke of Germany in the early part of 1970. Photo by Dieter Vogel.

The nine body bands are distinctly developed in this red discus.

A pair of breeding red discus. One of the fishes is concealed, except for part of its head and dorsal fin, behind the other.

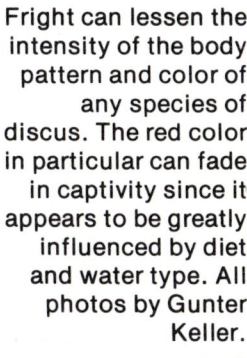

Fright can lessen the intensity of the body pattern and color of any species of discus. The red color in particular can fade in captivity since it appears to be greatly influenced by diet and water type. All photos by Gunter Keller.

WHERE DO DISCUS FISHES COME FROM?

The genus *Symphysodon* is confined exclusively to the South American continent, solely to the Amazon and its enormous tributary system. We can, therefore, regard Brazil, Peru, eastern Colombia, and perhaps Venezuela as the home of the discus fishes. More than 135 years have elapsed since a discus fish was first described, but where and how the discus fishes live has been found out only very recently. The Brazilian ethnologist Harald Schultz, known for his research on the Indians, who unfortunately died much too early, was one of the first who went on specific discus expeditions after World War II and brought back splendid specimens with good information on biotope and occurrence. Dr. Axelrod's ichthyological collection trips concerning the discus also yielded good results. But such knowledge as we may already possess on the ecology of these habitats we indisputably owe to Dr. Rolf Geisler. This scientist made several research journeys into the discus range. Today we already have some idea as to how the discus lives in its natural habitat, but we are still a long way from knowing all the answers, and much remains to be explored, collected, and examined.

To describe the Amazon with its tributaries as the range of the discus is really very vague. With its length of about 6,500 km and its gigantic tributaries—some of which reach a length of up to 3,000 km and are 10 km broad—this network of rivers covers an immense area. That certain species of fishes within this range are confined to particular localities is obvious. Equally obvious is that the information we have on the biotopes refers only to such fishing areas as we know of. This means that a lot more information can be expected in the future. From the description of localities, or waters, and coloration we can deduce that the different color varieties have only a local distribution.

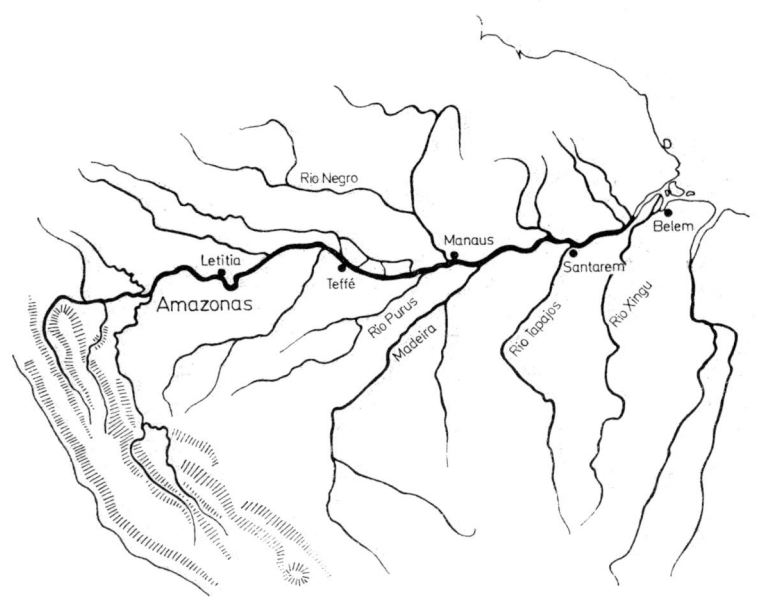

Shown are the areas of the Amazon River system where discus are taken.

Catches made in the area surrounding the town of Belem, for instance, which lies in the delta of the Amazon, are reported to yield only the brown discus. Whether these catches derive from the main stream of the Amazon is doubtful. On the contrary, it is much more likely that here, too, the discus is caught in the tributaries (and their tributaries), as e.g. in the Rio Xingu. Upstream, the next locality mentioned is the town of Santarem. Here is the estuary of the Rio Tapajos, and one can assume that, again, the catches stem from its tributaries. Brown and green discus are said to occur here. The richest localities are halfway up the Amazon. The collection and transfer point is the town of Manaus. The Rio Negro, which flows into the Amazon near Manaus, accommodates in its tributaries almost exclusively the "true discus," *Symphysodon discus* Heckel. This region has been thoroughly explored by Dr. Geisler. To all appearances, the occurrence of *Symphysodon discus* Heckel seems confined to the left tributaries of the Rio Negro. Its presence in the main stream seems unlikely. Presumably this goes for all discus localities. Farther upstream, up to and including the estuary of the Rio Purus, lies the locality in which the brown to blue discus is being caught. Mainly the "blue" to "royal blue" is found in the delta of the Rio Purus.

A native Brazilian from the Amazon who makes his living by catching discus for the commercial dealers of Manaus. Photo by Dr. Herbert R. Axelrod.

These photographs of the Amazon taken near Tefe depict the nature of "white waters." The water is turbid and almost opaque due to the presence of great amounts of silt. Photo by Dr. Herbert R. Axelrod.

Farther west, in the Lago Tefe, Harald Schultz caught green discus. It is highly likely that many more color variations can be found here. Very beautiful green discus are also being caught in Peru, near the town of Leticia. We can see how vast the area is in which the discus is caught and how little of it has actually been explored. Many a surprise may yet be in store for us.

With regard to most localities, we know that the discus fishes are not found in the actual stream or main river but in smaller tributaries, backwaters, and smallish lakes. These biotopes are characterized above all by a sometimes very slow current, a low water depth, and relatively steep banks with overhanging and partially immersed branches and roots. Precisely these characteristics describe the localities where the discus occurs. The fish seem to have a close attachment to the wood and are almost never seen anywhere but among the roots or among the tree-tops or branches that have fallen into the water. The water depth in these places is at least one meter and more. Owing to the color of the water, the dense branches (frequently with leaves), and the floating grass and leaves they are heavily shaded and relatively dark. Here the discus stand in schools of up to 50 fish. When disturbed, the whole school quickly dives and finds a good hiding place in the dark water among the root thickets.

I think it is justified to say that the discus, along with the neon tetra, has greatly influenced the evaluation and observation of water conditions in our aquaria. For many years, discus were very difficult to keep, so hobbyists paid a great deal of extra attention to the water. The research work of Dr. Sioli has given us very good insight into the water chemistry conditions of the Amazon tributaries holding discus. In the end, just about every aquarist had heard of the water of "Amazonia" as being very soft and acid. That we know still more about this water today we owe partly to Dr. Geisler. We know that the waters of "Amazonia" can be divided into three basic types. These are:

1. Streams with turbid, loamy water, called white waters.

2. Streams with clear, slightly greenish water—clean-water rivers.

3. Streams with clear but dark brown water, known as black waters.

These three water types develop due to different local geological and climatic conditions. The one thing they all have in common is their low mineral content. As compared to most American and European waters, their decisive difference is the well-nigh complete absence of dissolved calcium. Hence this water is very soft. Because they lack calcium with which carbon dioxide could form a bond, they are also acidic; humic acids are sometimes co-responsible for the low pH. The significance of these factors and their effect on the living processes of aquatic organisms were soon recognized, and today people try harder than ever to imitate these waters in the aquarium. We must be ready to admit, however, that these attempts will never be 100 % successful, and perhaps it is not necessary that they be. We must also beware of generalizations. Let us take the black-water type, for instance. There is a tendency to recommend this water for all tropical fishes, especially those from South America. For the discus it is said to be ideal. As a matter of fact, this black water is a very hostile environment for any form of life. Owing to the total lack of dissolved calcium and other minerals and the presence of a great deal of organic substance and of humic acids, the pH lies at around 4. This means the water is so acid that the animals fish feed on can barely live here, and larger fishes also find it difficult to survive. Discus fishes are inhabitants of white and clear water, but still more of mixed water. The Rio Negro, a typical black-water river, has large inflows of white water (Rio Branco) and clear water.

As already mentioned, the habitat of the discus often lies within the backwaters of such tributaries where the tributaries enter the

Discus find security among the bases of trees in an area like the one seen here. They are caught at night with the aid of a flashlight. Sudden light immobilizes the fish, momentarity giving an adept native collector time to scoop it up with his hand net. Photo by Dr. Herbert R. Axelrod.

Local settlements along the Rio Negro, a typical black-water river.

The bases of large trees along the banks of the Rio Negro are under water during flood conditions.

A view of an uninhabited section of the Rio Negro. The aquatic plants in the foreground are completely submersed during flood conditions. All photos by Dr. Herbert R. Axelrod.

Plastic-lined boxes being prepared for a fish shipment from the Amazon. Photo by Dr. Herbert R. Axelrod.

A section of the Rio Purus photographed by Harald Schultz. This river is the main habitat of the blue discus.

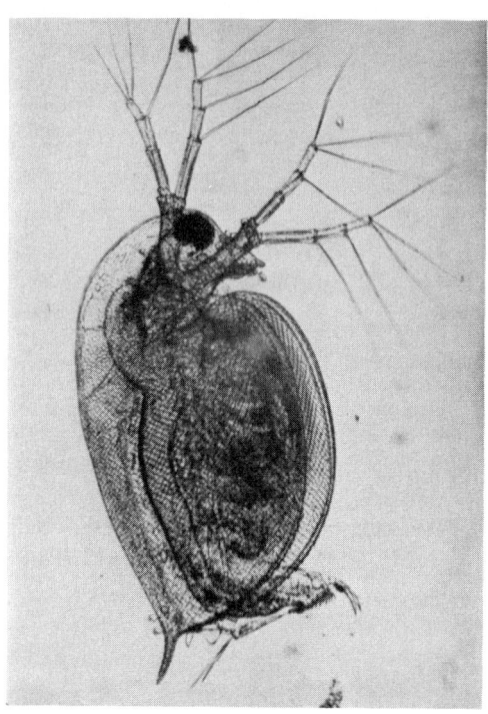

Although not the natural food of *Symphysodon*, *Daphnia*, along with other live foods, is accepted by them. Photo by Dr. Karl Knaack.

main stream. Color and composition of such mixed waters are subject to many changes and it is, therefore, virtually impossible to imitate them accurately. Within the Rio Negro range, however, depth visibility is better—as far as the mixed waters are concerned—than in those areas where the blue discus is being caught. The latter is collected mainly in the delta of the Rio Purus, where white water predominates. This water is very turbid and of a loam-yellow color. The turbidity is caused by mineral sediments which come from the Andes. Depending on the proportion of clear water that flows in, the depth visibility is sometimes no more than 25 cm. This type of water is not so acid (pH of up to 6.6) and its mineral content is slightly higher. Nevertheless, in this case, too, the water hardness is minimal and usually lies below 1 German degree. What all three types of water have in common is a relatively high iron content (usually around or above 1 mg/1) and a high proportion of organic substance. Presumably these factors are of great significance, too. The analyses of the waters in which discus fishes live all refer to shallow areas, however, for only these can be reached and examined. It is a known fact that during the rainy period the rivers and lakes rise by up to 16 m. Vast stretches of woodland are flooded at this time, and the water is bound to be changed. We can deduce from this that discus fishes are relatively adaptable (a look at our aquaria confirms this) and perhaps that they even need these changed conditions in order to reproduce themselves. But this is something we still need to look into. What is remarkable, however, is that from one fishing season to another animals of a fairly large and uniform size are caught, which means the animals must be growing very quickly and presumably do not spawn during the fishing season. Also connected with the variations of the water composition seems to be a fluctuation of the water temperatures. The waters of the Amazon range are relatively warm. From the very beginning, discus fishes in the aquarium have been kept at around 30° C. (86° F.) and this temperature is frequently encountered in natural discus waters as well. Interesting to note is the slight day-night fluctuation of the water temperature, which is usually less than 1° C. In tributaries of the Rio Negro, however, where *Symphysodon discus* Heckel occurred, Dr. Geisler observed a water temperature of 25° C. (77° F.). This was astonishing and once again shows how adaptable these fish are. Presumably the temperatures are slightly lower during the rainy period, when the water levels are so high, than they are during the warm drought. We need not worry, therefore, about subjecting our discus fishes to certain fluctuations of the water temperature, provided we don't make the changes too rapidly.

Still remaining of great interest is the quest for exact information on the natural diet of the discus fishes. The kinds of food we offer these fishes—e.g. *Tubifex, Daphnia*, enchytraeids, etc.—do not, or rarely, occur in the waters of the Amazon region. What the discus fishes live on can only be found out by examining the gastric contents of newly-caught specimens. However, this is difficult to do, all the more so since many of the fish are said to vomit up the contents of their stomach because of the shock of the capture. Nevertheless, Dr. Geisler has succeeded in answering this question. In the gastric contents and in the biotope of *Symphysodon discus* Heckel he has been able to observe the larvae of ephemerids (*Campsurus*). These insect larvae live in the leaf-covered bottom of the discus waters, and the fish rouse them by blowing against the bottom layer, then chase after them and swallow them. This blowing can often be seen in the aquarium when discus "dig up" a *Tubifex* worm that has almost buried itself in the bottom layer. A jet of water, spat out with considerable pressure behind it, sweeps away the sand or the leaf-mould and exposes the food animal. Along with the larvae of *Campsurus*, which sometimes occurred in enormous quantities, a small soft-shelled freshwater shrimp (*Macrobrachium*) was found. This diet of the discus was observed at a time when the water level was low in the discus

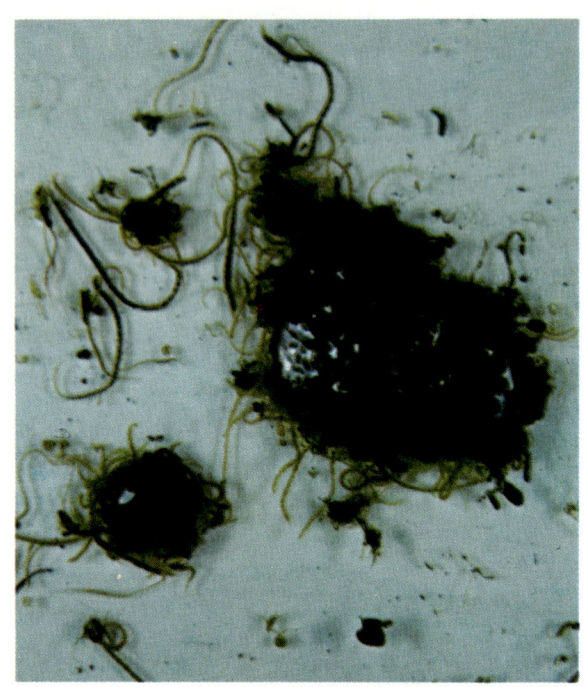

Two other kinds of food relished by discus are *Tubifex* worms (top photo) and enchytraeid worms (bottom photo). Photos by Charles O. Masters.

A Brazilian tropical fish collector with his family and boat.

With an improvised head lamp in place, this young man and his companion are getting ready for a typical night's work of collecting discus.

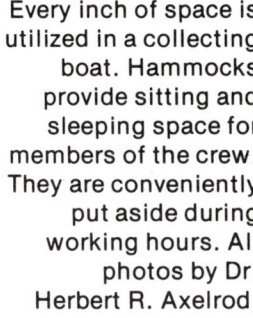

Every inch of space is utilized in a collecting boat. Hammocks provide sitting and sleeping space for members of the crew. They are conveniently put aside during working hours. All photos by Dr. Herbert R. Axelrod.

areas. What these fish feed on during the high water-level period—and above all what the fry eat—still needs to be found out. However, although the investigations by Dr. Geisler answer only a part of the question, they are still of great value to us.

Catching wild discus is a long, difficult job. As already mentioned, the town of Manaus is the point of departure for these expeditions and also the export center for discus fishes in Brazil. A few exporters have settled here, some of them with their own fishing fleets. The fishing areas of the "blue" and the "true" discus are roughly a two- to three-day boat journey away from Manaus. The fishing is done by native fishermen, some of whom have moved into houseboats within the fishing area. These fishermen have a good eye for the hiding places of the discus. With long nets, which are about 10 m long and 2 m broad, these sites (usually tree-tops that have fallen into the water) are enclosed in a semi-circle. Then the wood has to be taken out of the enclosure (a slow, difficult task), and then the net is dragged along the bottom and ashore. Frequently this entails several hours of labor and, owing to the turbid water, the result can only be seen at the very end. Then, long faces are often the only comment. A catch of fifty discus is a good result. Today the fish are stored and transported in baskets with a plastic lining. This has considerably reduced the danger of injuries, as compared to the oil barrels (cut open) that were used in the past. A total prevention of injuries can, of course, not be achieved, but the minor skin and fin injuries that do occur quickly heal in fresh water.

Discus are also caught at night. When it is dark the fish keep close to the surface, as can also be observed in the aquarium. These places are lit up with the aid of lanterns, and the startled animals are fished out with large hand nets. When enough have been caught the boat heads back for Manaus. On board, the water the discus are kept in is changed once a day and the containers are covered to protect them against the strong sunshine. At Manaus, the fish are stored in aquaria and plastic containers. While smaller fishes—above all characins—are already given dried food at this stage, it is doubtful that the wild discus would accept such food at this point, so they are shipped out as quickly as possible. According to their size, they are individually packed in plastic bags with oxygen. As a rule, two or three bags are used, as the discus can pierce single bags too easily with their hard fin rays. In addition, the whole thing is often wrapped in several layers of newspaper and then put into yet another plastic bag. Several of these bags are then packed into special Styrofoam boxes, and that is how discus set out on their long journey by air that eventually leads them into our aquaria.

DISCUS IN THE AQUARIUM

Thanks to modern methods of storage and transport, we now find a wide-ranging, good quality stock of discus for sale in pet shops. Some years ago, anyone who kept discus was still a true pioneer; often the animals (wild catches then) could be obtained only if one had special connections and was prepared to spend quite a lot of money. Today a large selection of both wild-caught and commercially raised discus waits for hobbyists who want them. There is no doubt that discus are still comparatively high-priced and, considering how difficult it is to breed them, this is not surprising. But nowadays no aquarist

For many years it was believed that one could keep discus only in a "hygienic" tank like the one shown here.

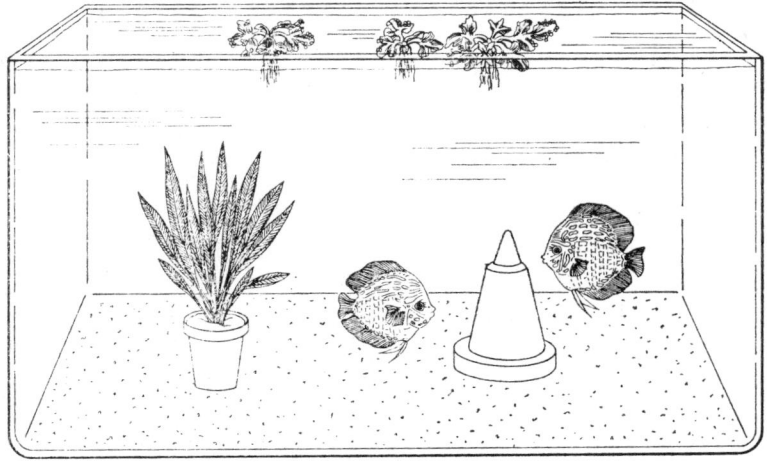

The bushy characteristic of the aquatic fern *Ceratopteris thalictroides* can provide the cover needed by shy and shade-loving discus. Photo by Dr. D. Terver, Nancy Aquarium.

Opposite:
Echinodorus paniculatus is a large species of Amazon sword plant that grows to a height of 5 feet, but in the confines of a tank and with a poor substrate its growth is retarded. Photo by Ruda Zukal.

41

should let himself be deterred from keeping discus as long as he is prepared to abide by a few basic rules, for it is no longer justified to describe discus as problem fishes. From our present day knowledge of the structure, behavior, and living requirements of these fishes we can adapt many procedures which ensure their successful keeping in the aquarium.

It is obvious that fishes measuring up to 20 cm in diameter and 2 to 3 cm in body thickness are quite large as aquarium fishes go and require accordingly large containers. How big a discus aquarium ought to be is difficult to say. There is certainly no upper limit, but it should by no means be smaller than 200 liters. Decisive factors are the number of fishes one intends to keep and how much time one is prepared to dedicate to the care of the water. Apart from the height of the tank (not below 50 cm), one should also take into consideration the size of the tank measured from front to back. It is the front-to-back dimension that provides the discus with room to swim, and it opens up various possibilities of decorating the tank. As a matter of fact, this is where the first conflict arises. For years it was considered necessary, if one wanted to keep discus successfully, to run a so-called hygienic aquarium. This is a bare aquarium, usually equipped with an up-ended flowerpot or similar object to serve as a hiding or spawning place, and probably a few floating plants. This functional set-up is designed above all to ensure cleanliness, specifically of the water. Food-remnants and feces remain visible and can be removed quickly. For the breeding tank, this type of interior can still be recommended today. But in a living room, for instance, an aquarium ought really to form part of the decoration, and for this such a bare and desolate glass box is definitely unsuitable. That is one reason why many aquarists have decided against keeping discus. However, experience has shown that there are other ways and that we need not be deprived of the so-called "aesthetic" aquarium after all. By "aesthetic" aquarium we mean a tank that can be considered an ornament and is decorated and planted according to the taste of its owner. The aesthetic aquarium is perfectly suitable for keeping discus, provided we do not make any fundamental mistakes and take certain factors into consideration.

From the description of the habitat of the discus fishes we can see that in the wild they are found in association with wood. This should be borne in mind, and safe wood should be used wherever possible. Wood in the form of the twisted roots of swamp trees is especially desirable, since it simulates the natural habitat. The bottom of the waters where discus fishes live is mostly sandy, dark and sometimes thickly covered with leaves. We should take the dark color into con-

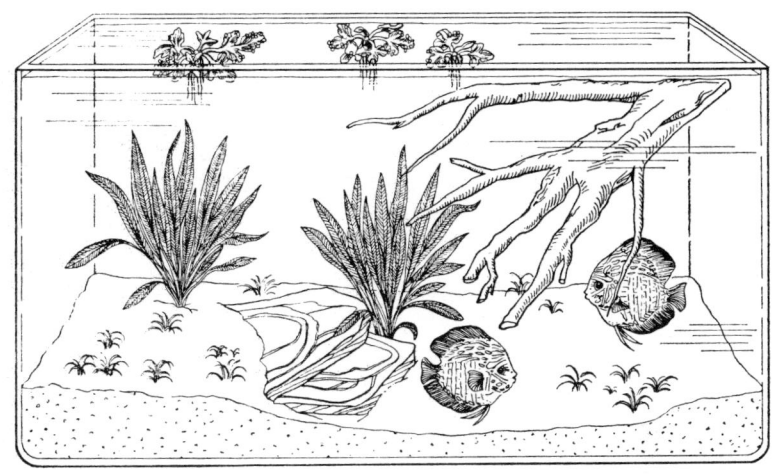

An "aesthetically" arranged aquarium provides the discus with hiding places and at the same time serves as a room ornament.

sideration and make sure that the bottom layer we provide does not contain too many soluble minerals or substances that tend to decompose.

The higher plants are absent from those parts of the rivers where discus are caught. This need not deter us, however, from inserting a few rooted plants, such as Amazon sword plants (*Echinodorus paniculatus, E. radicans*) or others, into the bottom layer. Every plant with a good growth has a beneficial effect on the water. A vital point to remember is to provide shading from above. The fish are used to semi-darkness, and a glaring light over the water surface can make them shy and colorless. A very suitable floating cover is provided by the water fern (*Ceratopteris*). This plant tolerates soft water, bright light and high temperatures very well, and its drooping roots make it look interestingly bizarre in the aquarium. A tank with this interior will fascinate every observer, and the fish have a chance to become acclimatized quickly and to revert to their original habits.

When choosing the bottom layer we have to make sure we are using the right material and that it does not absorb too much waste matter (feces and uneaten food). The latter can be prevented by care-

Some individual discus fish have red spots or speckles which further enhance their appearance. Photo by Gerhard Marcuse.

Opposite:
The red eye of this wild-caught discus is natural and not caused by injury. It was photographed close to the area of capture while still alive. Photo by Dr. Herbert R. Axelrod.

ful feeding and a relatively low fish population. In addition, the water in the aquarium should be filtered. The filter must be readily accessible so that it can be cleaned easily and frequently. What kind of filter one uses is not very important. All kinds and types of filters are being used by discus keepers, and all of them serve their purpose more or less equally well. The function of mechanical filters is to clear the water of turbidity caused by suspended substances. These filters have to be cleaned very often so that the dirt trapped by them does not re-enter the cycle. It is quite astonishing how quickly such a filter gets filthy. Alternatively, however, we could let a mechanical filter run as a biological filter. If this is intended, the filter medium should have a large surface, so we have to use something similar to coarse quartz gravel. Once the bacteria have begun to proliferate on the filter medium, the filter is an excellent aid to nitrification. This kind of filter should not be cleaned completely at frequent intervals, for cleaning destroys the active layer of bacteria and the filter becomes ineffective until new bacteria have accumulated on it. For the additional chemical treatment of the water one uses activated charcoal and peat. Activated charcoal is used for the extraction of chemicals, drugs, humic matter, and gases. As a permanent filter substrate, however, one cannot recommend charcoal without some reservation. It is true that the products of protein decomposition are trapped for a certain length of time, but it is very difficult to estimate when the maximum degree of adsorption will have been reached by the charcoal. Of course the overloaded charcoal filter still acts as a biological filter—if the water can flow through it freely—but for that we do not need charcoal. Charcoal, therefore, has to be replaced very often, and in the long run it is far from cheap. Peat, on the other hand, is a very useful material for the treatment of aquarium water. Peat-filtered water has proved excellent where the keeping of discus is concerned. Acid white peat is able, by combining with calcium, to de-harden the water and reduce its conductivity. By giving off humic acids, peat is able to lower the pH of water; it also increases its organic substance and gives the water a dark color. In this way we adapt our water to the natural water in which the discus live.

How big the individual filters have to be is difficult to say. It depends on the capacity of the aquarium, the properties of the water that is used, the fish population, and the constant maintenance of the water. The same goes for replacing the peat filter. As a rule of thumb one can say that for every 100 liters of water we need one-half to one liter of wet white peat which has to be replaced every four weeks. But it is important to check the reaction of the water. Very good results are achieved, in a larger tank, if a fast-running internal filter is equipped with nylon wool and a little peat and a large biological gravel filter is used in addition.

For very large tanks, power filters have proved excellent. In tanks with a capacity of below 300 liters however, power filters are less good because the discus don't like the strong current they produce, and we can observe how tense the fishes stand in the tank, trying to swim against the current. When the pump has been switched off they relax and swim normally, searching the bottom for food. This latter behavior is shown only when conditions in the aquarium are right for them.

WATER

The quality of the water has hitherto been regarded as being of primary importance in the keeping of discus. Today it is still widely held that discus can only be healthy—and therefore happy—in water which is absolutely perfect. This is not so. Naturally the fish are not comfortable in any old broth, and we certainly need to give as much attention to the water as it requires. But copying the natural Amazonian waters by using distilled or completely desalted water is quite unnecessary. The fishes tolerate medium-hard or even hard water perfectly well. Very few wholesalers or retailers offer the discus soft water, and the fishes show no adverse effects. There can be no doubt that it is better for the discus if we add fresh water of medium hardness from time to time rather than try to provide soft spring water. In this chapter I am presupposing that the discus fancier is familiar with such water chemistry terms as hardness, pH, conductivity, etc. Anyone wishing to go into this aspect in more detail will find good information in *Water Chemistry for Advanced Aquarists,* by Guido Huckstedt. This book also describes the equipment one requires to measure the properties of one's water prior to conditioning it. If we go by the natural discus waters, our water cannot be soft enough or acid enough. This type of water can be expensive to produce, however, and there are some inherent dangers (pH). Lucky is the hobbyist who gets soft water out of the tap. But not many are so lucky, and the great majority of aquarists have to adjust the water available to them. Many aquarists are in a position to obtain soft spring water, and such water can be considered ideal. It gets closest to the natural waters of the fish, as long as its conductivity (total salt content) and pH are similar too.

A suitable solution has been found in the partial desalting of raw water. Water with a carbonate hardness of two-thirds the total hardness can be easily and efficiently adjusted with the aid of weak ion-

Freshwater copepods like *Cyclops* are easy to collect from natural waters except during winter. Like most other fish fry, discus fry like them too.

Frozen bloodworms (*Chironomus*) are available in many aquarium fish shops. They are considered good, nutritious food for many fish species, including discus, when not fed heavily. Photo by Charles O. Masters.

The diet of discus can be supplemented occasionally by amphipods such as *Gammarus*. These can be eaten alive, but frozen ones are preferred. Apparently the chitin (shell) is somewhat softened during freezing. Photo by Charles O. Masters.

exchangers. By this process the calcium and magnesium ions are exchanged for carbon dioxide. Carbon dioxide quickly grows volatile, and one receives a water which is two-thirds softer. In a larger aquarium the water has to be well aerated, however, before this is done, or the fishes might die of asphyxiation due to an excess of carbon dioxide. Water with, for example, a total hardness of 15 German degrees and a carbonate hardness of 10 degrees has—after the exchange—a total hardness of no more than 5 German degrees. In water treated in this way and subsequently having a total hardness of 5 German degrees and a carbonate hardness of 1 degree, the wild-caught blue discus in my tank spawned six weeks after I had received them and propagated themselves normally.

Although discus still tolerate pH values down to 4.5, one should not go below a pH of 5; when the water is being changed and the peat filter removed, there is an especially great danger of acidosis. The best method of raising and stabilizing the pH is to add some raw water, provided the latter has a higher carbonate hardness.

It is important that the water not be allowed to become overloaded with the metabolic waste products of the fishes. The waste products, if present in excess, adversely affect the condition of the fish. In particular, growth is retarded, but there can be other negative effects such as general weakening and lower fertility. Here, the best method is to use a siphon and a bucket. A partial water change (one quarter of the tank capacity every two weeks) works like magic, and the fish reward us with their liveliness and their brilliant colors.

FOOD REQUIREMENTS

More important than anything else when we keep animals is to supply them with a correct diet. It was this aspect above all that seemed to make discus such a problem. Discus had the reputation of being extremely choosy fishes that would starve to death rather than take a monotonous diet. Today we know that fish which behave like this are diseased. But more about that later. Healthy discus are not choosy, eat readily, and always have a good appetite. Like most other cichlids, discus are fond of nourishing foods and of insect larvae in particular. Thanks to the gastric examinations by Dr. Geisler which I already mentioned, we know that ephemerids and certain freshwater shrimps are among the food animals taken by wild discus. These particular shrimps are almost impossible to obtain commercially, but that is no reason for us to give up. With the alternative foods available to us, discus can be fed and kept healthy for a long time. When I say "alternative foods," however, I do not mean the dry food that has proved of such value where other fish species are concerned. This is turned down by the discus. Only very young fish have a liking for it. But soon they too demand animal food, and we have to obtain live food for them. The selection is not all that limited, however. That ephemerids constitute part of the natural diet has already been mentioned. Instead of the soft-shelled shrimp *Macrobrachium*, one can offer *Gammarus pulex*, which is equally acceptable. Especially when they come from mountain or meadow brooks that have no fish life, amphipods are a valuable food, all the more so because they contain a lot of chitin; the chitin adds bulk and roughage to the food and hence is important for digestion. Unfortunately amphipods have somewhat hard shells, and it takes the fish some time to get used to this food. But if *Gammarus* are frozen after the catch and later

Giving your discus some larval mayflies will be a special treat for them. The natural food of wild discus includes ephemerids. Photo by Dr. Karl Knaack.

defrosted and given to the fish, they become softer. Then the discus swallow them more quickly and do not chew on them for so long.

Other very valuable foods are mosquito larvae (*Culex*) and glassworms (*Chaoborus*). When they are in season we should not fail to go around the ponds and collect them. Particularly in the pupal stage, they are a favorite food. In addition, they promote the growth of eggs in many fish species. Bloodworms (*Chironomus*) are another favorite and can be found in large numbers, especially in the winter. But this food can be dangerous. The larvae can be found in the most polluted of waters and may carry a variety of fish-pathogenic organisms or dangerous chemicals. In fact, fish mortalities are not unusual when large quantities of these larvae have been fed to the fish. In addition, the biting apparatus of these larvae can cause injuries inside the stomach of the fish if the larvae have been swallowed whole, and this may cause further mortalities. This risk can be eliminated by feeding

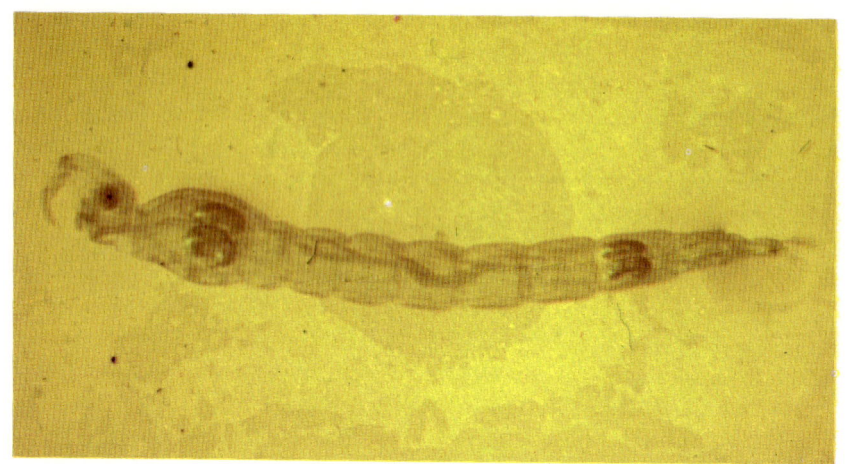

Glassworms are larval forms of *Chaoborus*. These are insects related to mosquitoes but are incapable of sucking blood. Photo by Dr. Rolf Geisler.

Enlarged photograph of a typical mosquito larva. During the warm months of the year larval mosquitoes are very easily collected in standing pools and lakes. They can also be cultured in special containers. Adults should not be allowed to escape. Photo by Dr. Rolf Geisler.

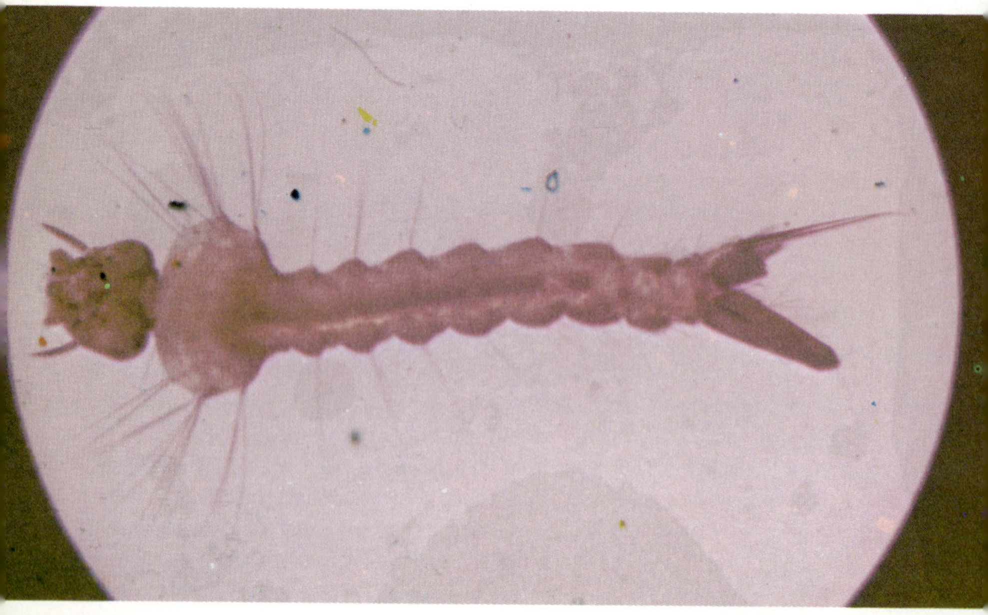

Mouth-to-mouth confrontation is normal for many members of the family Cichlidae. The activity illustrated here by discus never seems to end tragically. It is just a means of establishing either the dominant or the subservient role of an individual fish. Photo by Hans J. Mayland.

frozen bloodworms. All the food animals mentioned so far can be stored in this way. This enables us, particularly during the winter months, to supply our fish with biologically valuable food. That this food has to be defrosted before use goes without saying. If it is not, it can cause inflammations of the stomach and the intestine.

The main food of many discus in our aquaria, and one that is popular with them, is the *Tubifex* worm. But *Tubifex* presents much the same problem as bloodworms. *Tubifex* occur almost exclusively in waste-waters or in brooks with a high content of organic matter. *Tubifex* also harbors many harmful substances in its intestine and other organs. The worms therefore have to be washed thoroughly. It should also be avoided to feed *Tubifex* to the virtual exclusion of all else. Such an unbalanced diet upsets the digestion of the fish and results in diarrhea.

Somewhat more advantageous are the enchytraeids. These home-bred worms are a very nutritious food and should, therefore, be given only in modest amounts. That much-feared fatty degeneration of the fish only sets in if enormous quantities of these worms are fed to them. Three to four enchytraeid meals a week—especially when the fish are still growing—can be considered safe and beneficial. Enchytraeids as a food have the advantage that they can be washed and enriched with added vitamins.

Minced beef heart has proved to be another good substitute for the discus natural fare. All fat and fiber are removed from the meat, which is then minced or chopped finely, or—if it is frozen—grated with a kitchen-grater. Once the fish have grown accustomed to this food they develop a liking for it and, as far as I know, it has no adverse effects. On the contrary, this food can be conveniently enriched with the vitamin preparations available on the market and so becomes an excellent addition to the menu.

Suitable for the fry are water-fleas (*Daphnia*), Grindal worms, *Cyclops* and brine shrimp (*Artemia*). The young fish also take freeze-dried foods (whole animals or tablets) and flaked foods. When they can be seen to nibble at soft water plants, feeding with frozen spinach may be indicated. For constant variety in their bill of fare our pets reward us with their quick growth and vitality.

HINTS ON KEEPING

Their size limits the number of discus we can keep, and it also makes them undesirable for the so-called community tank. Added to this, their secretive and secluded way of life in their native biotope leads one to assume that they are not fond of too much company. It is true that when wild discus are caught the net frequently contains angelfishes and other cichlids along with them, but discus really look best when kept by themselves. Five or six animals always form an attractive group and bring enough life into any tank. Their color and shape make them such a center of attraction that contrast fishes become unnecessary. But that is a matter of personal taste and should be left for the individual aquarist to decide. It is important, however, to be aware of the danger of infection the discus would be exposed to if they were constantly subjected to the company of other species. Many ornamental fishes are carriers of parasitic diseases without themselves showing any signs of sickness. Such fishes tolerate their own parasites fairly well but invariably infect discus. Angelfish in particular are a great source of danger in this respect, and constant observation becomes imperative.

We are lucky in that discus are very peaceful cichlids. They do not attack other fish, except perhaps—but very rarely—the odd small fry (food fishes), and leave the plants where we put them. They can, however, become very shy and nervous if exposed to the wrong environmental conditions. The latter include glaring lights (shading and dark corners have been mentioned), the sudden appearance of shadows in the aquarium, vibrations, and—above all—a worsening of the water quality. The latter—due to drugs, the wrong pH, and pollution—is easy to remedy. It is, however, possible that this flight behavior is normal. If the tank provides hiding places similar to those occurring in the natural habitat of the discus, then the fish hurriedly retreat to them whenever they feel threatened. This behavior is particularly common in "adolescent" animals.

If we keep the discus under the good conditions mentioned so far, they will give us much pleasure, and we will have the opportunity to study their many modes of behavior and to see our pets grow and reproduce.

An inverted flowerpot is an ideal substrate for laying the eggs. This pair of breeding blue discus is watching over the clutch of eggs. Photo by Dr. Eduard Schmidt-Focke.

Opposite:
A pair of breeding brown discus guarding their spawn deposited on the vertical side of a concrete building block. Infertile eggs become fungused and appear opaque. Photo by Dr. Herbert R. Axelrod.

BREEDING DISCUS

Healthy and well-nourished discus may be able to reproduce at the age of about 12 months. But to achieve this, they have to be fed very well and must be raised under optimal conditions. Aquarists who feed their animals only twice a day are hardly likely to receive sexually mature fish within the year. It is, therefore, not uncommon to observe that under normal conditions one and a half to two years elapse before discus start to reproduce. This delightful and important event announces itself a few days in advance and, if the animals are closely observed, can be noted in good time. Unfortunately we are still not able to distinguish the sexes of discus by any external characteristics. In the past there have been many references to structural differences concerning the body, fins, and lips which were interpreted as sex differences (e.g. saddlenose, pointed anal and dorsal fins, separated rays of the ventral fins, and thick lips). From the earliest days of discus-keeping one also believed differences in color to be relevant in the differentiation of the sexes. Today we know that none of the color shades or variations are limited to either sex. It can be observed, however, that the male of a breeding pair is slightly larger and more thick-set as a rule. Where the "royal blue" color variety is concerned, the males often show stronger markings, and their colors also are more intense. But this is not the general rule, and these characteristics have only a limited part to play in the correct determination of the sexes.

With young fish it is definitely impossible to distinguish the sexes with any degree of certainty. One is obliged, therefore, to acquire a number of individuals and leave it to the fish to find each other and get paired off. Before they do so one can observe that a certain hierarchy has established itself in the discus tank. The biggest and most energetic fellow dominates the others absolutely and constantly defends the feeding place. Then come successively subordinate grades, right down to the last in the pecking order—and that one is pushed around by everyone. Usually this is the smallest fish. Although it always has a good appetite, it is hardly allowed near the food without being dealt a few blows. That such animals show a retarded development is not surprising. Since this pecking order is constantly being put to the test and re-arranged, some hobbyists have been inclined to use it as another aid to sex determination. Fish which were always on the offensive or warded off a head-on collision by lashing out with their tails were thought to be males, while obviously submissive fish were considered to be females. This submissiveness or inferiority was demonstrated by decoloration, prominence of the nine cross bands, retraction of the fins, and flight. But this behavior is not confined to a particular sex. It is true that in most cases the fish at the very top of the hierarchy is a male, but there are exceptions to this rule.

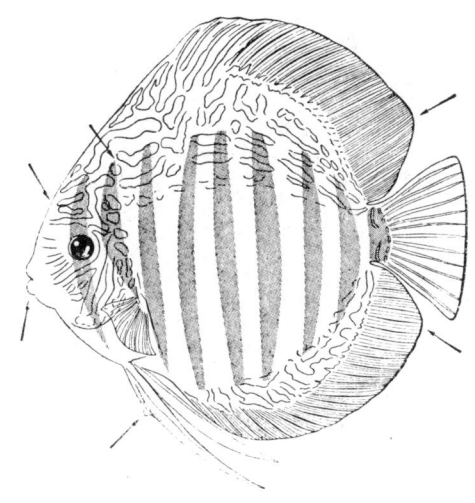

The sexes in discus are difficult to distinguish. Arrows point to areas of the body that are often mentioned to show sex differences. These are, however, questionable. (See the text.)

When two fish are "making eyes at each other," their mutual attacks markedly decrease, and they often stand together. Courtship begins with the two fish inclining the head slightly as they swim towards each other and literally making a bow. This bow is accompanied by a quick splaying and retracting of the tail fin. At the same time the head usually grows dark in color while the body grows lighter, and the tail fin comes to look soot-black. The male takes the main initiative. Simultaneous with this behavior is a twitching of the dorsal fin. If the female is ready to spawn, it replies with the same signals, and soon after the well-known "cichlid-shaking" can be seen. This "shaking" is a horizontal to-and-fro movement carried out with

A pair of breeding brown discus photographed in a display tank at Nancy Aquarium, France. Photo by Dr. D. Terver.

A close-up view of the eggs. Except for two or three opaque eggs, all appear to be in very good condition. Photo by Dr. D. Terver, Nancy Aquarium, France.

A turquoise discus with a swarm of fry along the sides of the body. These young are actually feeding on the body secretion of the parent fish. Photo by Hans J. Mayland.

the front part of the body by each partner in turn. At this stage the animals choose a spawning site and then proceed to polish whatever objects happen to be there.

This is usually a moment of conflict for the discus-keeper. Should he take out the potential spawners and transfer them to a breeding aquarium? Or should he leave them in the show tank and take out the other fish? Often one is quite unprepared for this situation, and another aquarium is not always available. Then the hobbyist has no choice but to stand back and see what happens. The removal of the other fish would cause the least disturbance to the breeders. There have also been instances, however, when broods were raised in the presence of other discus. But this usually results in a certain amount of chaos, and the risk of failure is high. In a large show tank it invariably becomes a problem to feed the fry, and not many of them are likely to survive into adulthood.

One is well-advised, however, to let the fish spawn in their familiar surroundings for the time being and to watch what is going on. In this way one can find out a) whether the "newly-weds" really are male and female, b) whether they get along with each other, and c) whether the eggs have been fertilized. There have been enough occasions when two animals of the same sex showed the most convincing mating behavior but, after they had rashly been separated from the other animals, presented the greatest difficulty when the aquarist tried to "breed" them.

In their natural environment, discus presumably deposit their spawn on submerged trees or roots. If available, the same spawning substrate is chosen in the aquarium, but discus also select large stones, large plant leaves, the glass panes of the aquarium, or the heater or thermostat, etc. The chosen spawning site is freed from algae, dirt, and slime. The broad-leaved plants suffer most in this respect; often they are seriously damaged by the vigorous cleansing activity of the fish. The chances of a good result are slim when the eggs have been deposited on leaves. Over the years, flowerpots or vases made of clay have become firmly established as spawning substrates. This method has proved particularly successful in the "hygienic" breeding aquaria described earlier. Usually when the spawning pair is fished out of the show tank and transferred to this type of breeding tank, their breeding instinct is interrupted. The fish need some time to get used to their new surroundings; luckily, though, in most cases the mating urge soon returns. This kind of tank, which need not be too large (150 to 200 liters), offers the best guarantee for successful breeding. As a rule, the animals spawn in the evening, irrespective of whether the light is on or not. At this time it becomes possible to determine the sexes by observing the structure of the genital papilla. The female's ovipositor protrudes noticeably more and its breadth appears to remain constant. In the male, on the other hand, the genital papilla narrows down like a cone. At this stage the color of the fish also changes. They may grow so dark as to appear almost black. Only the caudal peduncle sometimes remains light. This coloration is most marked during the actual act of spawning. It must be added, however, that it is not of the same intensity in all discus and all varieties. Nor does the color give us any indication as to whether the parents are likely to care for their brood or not. To lay the eggs, the female approaches the spawning site from below. She retracts her fins and the eggs emerge like a string of pearls. The eggs are slightly yellowish and have a diameter of about 1 mm.

This is where the up-ended flowerpot proves invaluable. Owing to its relatively large surface area, the discus female can spread out each egg-chain and leave a greater space between them. This is an advantage, for if the eggs die and grow mycotic, the parent animals remove them. But with their large mouths they invariably damage the eggs close by, and what they end up destroying sometimes outweighs the intended improvement. If the eggs lie on a narrow branch or leaf or some equally small space, they are very close together and frequently piled on top of each other as well. In this case the losses caused by the parents when they try to pick out the bad ones are particularly high.

The male fertilizes each egg-chain as soon as it has been laid, always giving the impression of sizing up the eggs with its "nose" before it swims across them and distributes the spermatozoa. As a rule the act proceeds as described. It is accompanied by severe "shaking" of both fish. It can also happen, however, that both partners carry out their functions simultaneously. Equally possible, unfortunately, is that the female lays her eggs and the male shows no interest in breeding or is distracted by an observer. We should then get away from the tank and leave the fish to themselves. Often we are forced to watch how certain males leave the eggs unfertilized and quickly swallow them.

The number of eggs depends on the condition, nutrition, and size of the parents. Wild catches not infrequently produce 300 to 400 eggs per clutch, but 200 is a good average. When spawning is over each animal by turn fans the eggs with its pectoral fin, thereby supplying them with water which has a high oxygen content while at the same time removing dirt particles and small organisms from them. Often the first problem of discus breeding arises at this stage: a wrong reaction by one or both of the parents when engaged in caring for the

Larger fry can stray some distance from the parent as they get older. Although capable of feeding on other foods offered, they still instinctively return to the parent. Photo by Dr. Eduard Schmidt-Focke.

brood. Very often one can now observe the eating of the eggs for which discus are notorious. One partner shows itself unwilling to look after the brood, pushes the "nursing" animal away from it, and proceeds to swallow the eggs. This behavior is not confined to the discus alone but can be observed in other cichlids as well. The angelfish is perhaps the greatest expert in this respect, which explains why it is almost always reared artificially. How the eating of the eggs can be prevented we do not know. Many experiments have been carried out using different methods, but none proved successful. In many cases we are lucky and things simply sort themselves out. After having eaten its previous clutches, a pair may suddenly look after its latest brood with the utmost care. Notably the young fish show a marked tendency to indulge in egg-eating. Here the aquarist must keep his nerve and exercise great patience. Should the abnormal behavior persist over a longer period, then the fish are unsuitable for breeding to each other and must be exchanged. Often there is instant success with the new partner.

The key to success in breeding discus is to have a pair of fish that take good care of the brood. This need not necessarily be the pair which originally found one another. Often the dominant males are the first to get a female to spawn, but then they show their wicked nature. It is preferable, therefore, always to keep a number of animals so that changes can be made. It should not be necessary to point out how important it is to feed the animals well when they get ready to spawn. Particularly suitable at this time are insect larvae, and an occasional dose of vitamin enriched food can be recommended, too. To some extent, this will also help to reduce the parents' appetite for their eggs.

Let us return to the normal, however. Here we see one fish, often both, engaged in fanning the eggs. The head is light-colored now, almost yellowish, and the body dark. This characteristic "nursing color" is not always fully displayed, however. Perhaps this is due to the aquarium and its own surroundings, making it difficult for the fish to 'find themselves' and develop their full natural behavior.

Kept at a temperature of 28-30° C, the brood hatches within 50-60 hours. Often they are assisted by their parents, who suck them out of the egg cases and then attach them to another part of the spawning substrate. At this stage the larvae are not yet able to swim and derive the necessary nourishment from their vitelline sac. The larva has three pairs of glands on the head which secrete a mucous substance by means of which the larva becomes attached to objects. This secretion is vital; without it, the larva would sink to the bottom of the dark waters in its natural habitat and inevitably perish. But because of it,

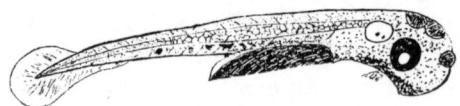

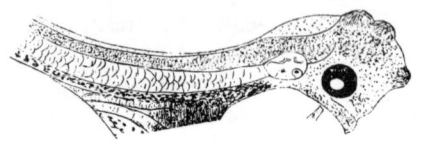

Head glands of young (upper) and older (lower) discus larvae. (After Wickler.)

the parent animals can deposit their brood on a suitable surface and constantly keep an eye on them. Larvae which wriggle themselves free and sink to the bottom are caught with the mouth and spat back in their place. Again the flowerpot, with its sloping sides and the rim where the larvae become attached, proves highly suitable.

I should mention here that at this stage the aquarium must be scrupulously clean and that above all the water must be in good condition, i.e. low in bacteria and not saturated with waste matter. This is best achieved with the peat filter described earlier. Another good aid is a UV-filter, particularly where we wish to combat water turbidities caused by bacteria. Nursing pairs are now very busy with their young and transfer them to another locality from time to time. At this time we have to choose the parents' food with extra care. Generally speaking, anything that wriggles should be avoided, for in most cases this kind of food is misidentified by the parents and spat in the same place as the wriggling brood. Whole bunches of larvae which then become attached to, say, a *Tubifex* worm can sink as a result and be lost. To avoid this risk, it is best to give frozen food to the animals. This food does not move and is swallowed without hesitation.

The larval stage lasts three to four days; then the brood begins to grow independent. We have now come to another decisive phase. The wriggling movements of the larvae have gained in intensity over the last few hours, and the first larvae now succeed in detaching themselves from the spawning substrate and swim off immediately. The first of the escapees are recaptured by the parents and spat back in their place, but usually they set off again straight away, and the numbers of larvae swimming towards their parents are constantly growing. The latter give up their hopeless attempts to keep the brood together and—very dark in color now—quietly stand in front of the brood. As is well known, discus emit a skin secretion which serves as nourishment for the young for the first few days after they have become able to swim actively. Often this secretion can be seen before the larvae swim free, when it forms the milky-gray deposit on the back of the parent animals.

This skin secretion is vital for the young, as they do not ingest any other food for at least the first two to four days. How the young find their way to the source of nourishment is still not known. Normally, the brood swims towards the parents by the shortest possible route and proceeds to "graze" on the secretion, usually starting on the head and the back and then working onto the dorsal fin. Scent and

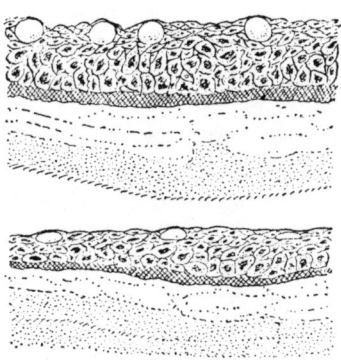

Cross-section through the skin and scales of a brooding (upper) and a "normal" (lower) discus. One sees the large mucous glands (white) lying below the upper surface of the much thickened skin. Outside of the brooding time the skin is thinner and the mucous glands in the epidermis are small. (After Hildeman.)

optical signals are thought to be responsible for the tracking down of the food source. But there have also been occasions when whole broods could be observed to swim past the parent animals although the skin secretion was clearly visible. If the young fail to find the way to the parent animals within the shortest possible time, they invariably perish. They stray around the aquarium for a few more hours and then disappear. Usually the animals try very hard to keep the brood at the food source. Escapees are carefully pursued and caught with the mouth. The young fish is chewed briefly and spat out again. As a rule it then swims towards the parent animal without delay and joins its siblings which are busy feeding. For the first few hours both parents offer themselves to the brood as "grazing grounds."

Later, however, one animal detaches itself from the brood by suddenly swimming off very quickly, and the young change over to the other parent. After a short time—seconds to minutes later—the first animal swims to the partner with the young and, by twitching its fins, lures the brood towards it. The released fish, in turn, swims off now and takes a break. Since the great majority of the brood start to swim in the morning, they have practically all day to stuff themselves with food. Towards the evening, many discus pairs gather their young together again by picking them up and spitting them back into the spawning place. Here the young re-attach themselves to the mucus threads still present and spend the night just as they did during the larval stage. This behavior can not be observed in all animals, however. Often the parent animals can be seen to leave the brood on their bodies, making no attempt to collect the young. Where this is the case we should leave a weak light on during the night. If one suddenly turns off the light, it will not be long before the young start to wander through the tank, and by morning there may already be fewer of them, or the ties with their parents will have been severed, causing the fry to flee. It is advisable to leave on a weak lamp over the spawning place for the first two nights after the young have become able to swim.

When the brood is grazing on the body of a parent animal, evidence of the food intake can already be seen a few hours later. By this time the bellies of the young have grown bigger and are visibly filled with a white mass. At this stage one can say that the major obstacle in discus breeding has been overcome. But there may be a few more difficulties yet, for the eggs are not the only thing the parent discus can show themselves partial to. A similar phenomenon can also be found during the larval stage of the young, and at the end of a quarrel in front of the brood it often happens that the whole brood is swallowed. Such animals tend to indulge themselves again if they get the chance and have to be watched very carefully. If they repeat this behavior several times, we have to exclude them from breeding. Fortunately they are in the minority. More common, on the other hand, is a quarrel over who carries the young. The partner who is carrying them feels reluctant to change over again and would like to keep them. Then we can witness proper scenes of jealousy which are accompanied by attacks and biting. This is not good for the young fish; they now cling so tightly to the parent animal they happen to be with that they are prevented from feeding. Often each parent animal has some of the young and tries to lure the rest away from its mate. The strong twitching of the fins puts the fry into a state of alarm and they nestle up to the parent and keep perfectly still.

These occasional rows can be regarded as normal marital quarrels, and we should not interfere. But if an individual fish makes trouble all the time, constantly attacking its partner and even taking out its bad temper on the young by snapping at them, it is often better to separate the pair. The parent the young are with most of the time should be left in the tank and the other fished out. Although breeding success is in doubt now, the risk of failure was much greater while the two parents were fighting. Fish which previously showed themselves reluctant to hand over the young to their mate often continue to look after the brood on their own. Usually their supply of skin secretion is adequate, too. The brood must have been feeding on the skin secretion for at least two days before we can hope to keep them alive on some sort of substitute food. But even then the result is far from good, and if the young survive they grow very slowly. For this reason, attempts have been made to raise discus fry artificially. The "nutrient slime" of discus was carefully analyzed. It was thought the secretion also served as a culture medium for protozoans which then formed the primary nourishment of the grazing discus fry. But apparently this is not so, because the examined slime was free from unicellular organisms.

In the United States lots of attempts are still being made to raise and feed discus artificially. Recipes for this are said to be available, at considerable prices. Good results with artificial rearing methods seem to have been achieved by Jack Wattley in Florida, for example, but he keeps his methods secret. Carroll Friswold consistently succeeded in raising discus fry artificially, and an account of his method can be found in *All About Discus*, by Dr. Herbert R. Axelrod and others.

How important the skin secretion is can be seen from the fact that in the early stage the young almost double their body length from day to day. If the parent animals look after their brood peacefully, the fry have constant access to this nourishment and can be seen to graze without interruption. Sometimes the "slime" seems to be a bit on the tough side, and one can observe that the young really have to tug at it and twist it around before they manage to tear off their mouthful. Four to six days may elapse before it becomes necessary for us to offer any supplementary food to the fry. Dependence on the skin secretion (and thus on the parents) is so strong at first that the young do not go after free-swimming food. We cannot do better than to start off with live baby brine shrimp, an ideal supplementary food. The young discus chase after these nauplii even after they are well past the fry stage. When we feed the fry with *Artemia*, it is an advantage to use a smallish breeding tank with a smooth bottom. In this way the animals can find all the nauplii they have been given, including those which are already half-dead and lying on the bottom. In a large, decorated tank this would not be so easy.

When we start to feed the young on regular foods, we need to change the water at frequent intervals, and this also promotes good growth. A powerful filter should, of course, not be connected to the aquarium during the first few days of independent swimming. Many a discus brood has been known to vanish inside of one.

Once the fry have started to accept a supplementary food we no longer need to be so particular about keeping the water hardness very low. Of course we should continue to check the pH and to make sure that it does not rise above 7. Owing to the large supplies of food in a small space, the decomposition of proteinic substances could well result in the formation of ammonia.

Another suitable food that ensures good growth is Grindal worms. These food animals can be mashed and enriched with added vitamins, as I pointed out earlier. Although the young fish are now at the stage where they derive most of their nourishment from live food, they still continue to swim to the parents for more of the skin secretion. Sometimes they actually go so far as to injure the skin and eat holes into it. The skin tissue seems to taste particularly good. Now it is high time to separate the young from their parents. Generally speaking, one should leave the baby fish with their parents for three to four weeks. How much the skin secretion taken in addition to live food promotes growth is obvious. At this age they already take almost anything they can swallow. They eat *Cyclops*, small water fleas, finely-chopped *Tubifex*—and beef heart as well. This is also the time when we can introduce them to dry food. Experiments with mixed foods containing agar have also proved very successful. These foods were made up of calf's liver and spleen, water fleas, mosquito larvae, and a variety of commercial dry foods, turned into a mash in the mixer and bound with agar-agar.

Young discus are temperamental and forever hungry. Even when they are no bigger than the size of a thumbnail, they fight over bits of food. They should, therefore, be fed several times a day. In this way they grow better, and they also have a greater resistance to diseases. They definitely should have variety in their diet.

As soon as the young fish are 4 to 5 cm long—and I am here referring to the blue, turquoise, and green varieties—the first touch of color can be seen. On the head, the back, and the anal fins they show a blue-green sheen. This is no indication of the final color, however. What this is to be only becomes apparent after a year or so, and it takes two to three years for the coloration to be completed, notably with regard to its intensity. Contrary to these experiences, one can sometimes see young discus with a length of up to 5 cm which have an intense red-blue-green color. They look almost unnaturally colorful,

A true discus and its large brood of young. At this stage the young should be fed well to ensure normal development. Photo by Dr. Eduard Schmidt-Focke.

and this in fact is what they are: *unnaturally* colorful. The majority of such discus come from Southeast Asia, where discus are dyed by ingenious breeders and exporters. The fry are given a food to which dyes and—above all—hormones have been added. Sex hormones in particular lead to this striking coloration that we normally find only in sexually mature animals, though not at this intensity. Whether such methods can harm the fish is not known, but it seems far from impossible. However, since the exporters describe these fish as dyed, one cannot accuse them of fraud. Unfortunately, not all of the people who know that the fish they're selling have had their colors artificially enhanced or induced bother to tell their customers. Whether a discus fancier should acquire artificially colored fish is a matter of taste. But it needs to be said that the striking color disappears as soon as the special food is discontinued. I would consider it much more rewarding to watch a small shoal of well-cared for young fish develop their natural colors.

But the color is not the only thing that matters. Healthy growth (with length and height being at the correct proportion) and a beautiful development of the fins are more important, where the appearance of discus is concerned, than an oblong splash of color. Furthermore, it would be wrong to cross all the discus variations with each other just for the sake of success. While it seems likely that the colors of the blue and green varieties could be further intensified through selective breeding, it would be still more rewarding if we could succeed in getting above all the full-color quality to be genetically transmitted. Regrettably, however—owing to the relatively long time-lag between generations, the non-identifiability of the sexes, the late completion of its coloration, and the complicated raising of the young —the discus is not ideally suited for this type of project. Nevertheless, we can be certain that many attempts will be made to reach this goal, since many skilled aquarists are filled with enthusiasm for discus.

Angelfish and discus are compatible fishes; they eat the same type of food and require similar tank conditions. Here they are being fed live *Tubifex* worms.

DISEASES

The diseases to which they are subject are one big reason why discus have always been considered to be a problem fish. It took some years for the problems to be identified and, with the aid of science, gradually to be cleared up. Many aquarists have already been forced to look on helplessly as the discus in their aquaria grew apathetic, refused all food, and then slowly but surely died. All the tricks that could be thought of were tried, but in the end it had to be admitted that the fish were suffering from diseases for which there was no known cure. If today we are able to look to the future a little more optimistically, special credit for this must go to Dr. Gottfried Schubert of Hohenheim University. Also of great value to aquaristics were the works by Prof. Reichenbach-Klinke, by Dr. Herckner, by Dr. Amlacher, and many others. They have carried out intensive research into the diseases of the discus and were able to supply much valuable information. Dr. Schubert has dedicated himself particularly to public work; he examined hundreds of discus for aquarists and looked for the causes of the diseases. He has developed many methods of investigation and treatment and published them in essays and lectures. Mortalities will continue to occur, but we have much cause to be satisfied with what has been achieved and can now already do quite a lot to nurse our pets back to health. A few good drugs have also been developed which assist us in this task.

Discus can contract a great variety of diseases. Since a fish, like other animals, is able to cope with a certain number of parasites, it may be diseased without this becoming apparent to us. The first signs of ill health are reflected in color changes and behavior changes. Good observation is, therefore, always essential. Unfortunately we seldom get hold of discus that are free of parasites. Wild-caught discus in particular are often infested with tapeworm larvae and other parasites. The emphasis in caring for the discus, therefore, must be placed on the providing of natural conditions so that we help to build up the resistance of the fish. This still applies today, despite our ability to treat the worst diseases by direct methods. Below, I am describing the diseases that most commonly affect discus kept in the aquarium.

ACIDOSIS

Water which is too acid can cause severe damage to the fish. Where we have very soft water in combination with peat filtration, the risk of acidosis is highest. Affected fish grow dark in color and seem reluctant to swim. Often, however, they may shoot through the tank as if panic stricken. After prolonged exposure to excessively acid water the skin shows patches of milky turbidity and the formation of thickened white areas can be seen. One should not allow the pH to drop below 5.

Treatment: Instant raising of the pH by changing the water, using a new water having a higher alkalinity and carbonate hardness. Commercial products designed to alter the pH are also available.

A histological section of the skin with several *Costia* attached.

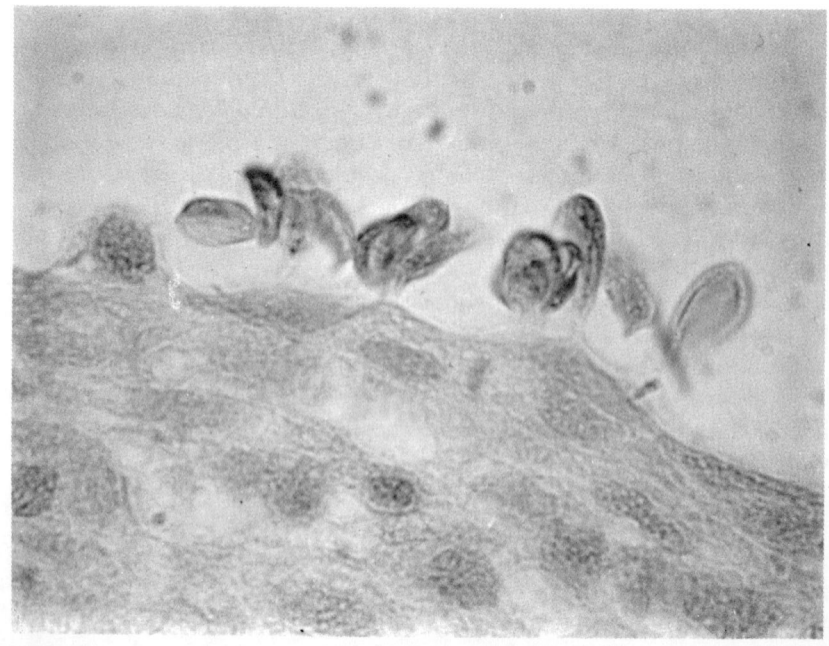

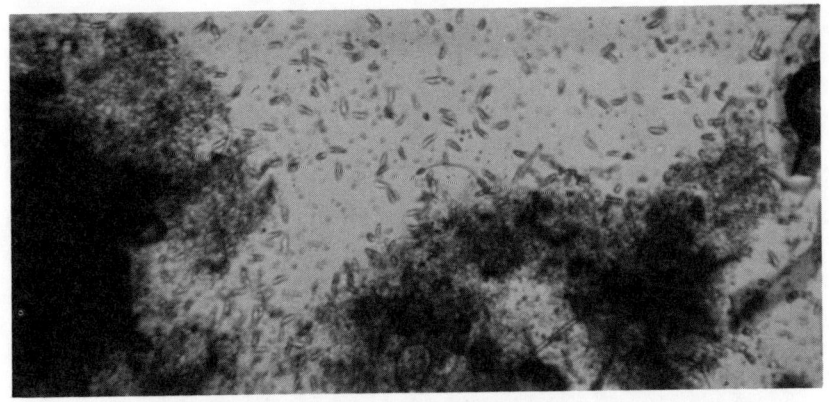

Infusoria photographed under low magnification of a microscope. Other fishes may eat these organisms, but they have harmful effects on discus.

SKIN IRRITATION

Discus react very strongly to infusorians in the aquarium water. Again the fish grow very dark, almost black, twitch their fins very frequently, and swim with sudden abrupt movements. Often the skin comes to look rough and spotty. If the water is examined under a microscope, countless tiny organisms can be seen. First of all one has to find out why the infusoria have developed (uneaten food, dead plants, etc.). Cleaning of the filter is advisable. If the infusoria persist, the water can be treated with bacterial agents like acriflavine, used in accordance with the manufacturer's directions.

SKIN TURBIDITY

Where skin and fins of the discus show a gray deposit—usually clearly visible owing to the dark coloration of the fish at such times—they are likely to be infested with protozoans. The latter may be skin flagellates of the genera *Costia, Chilodonella,* or *Trichodina,* or belong to an *Oodinium* species. These parasites also attack the gills and cause the fish to breathe faster. Infected fish usually retract the fins and scrape themselves on firm objects. A precise diagnosis is possible only with the aid of skin smears under the microscope. For this, we have to consult the special literature. However, since a great variety of causative agents can be controlled with the same drugs, commercial treatments are generally applicable in such cases. Treatment is best carried out in the aquarium. To prevent the plants from being

75

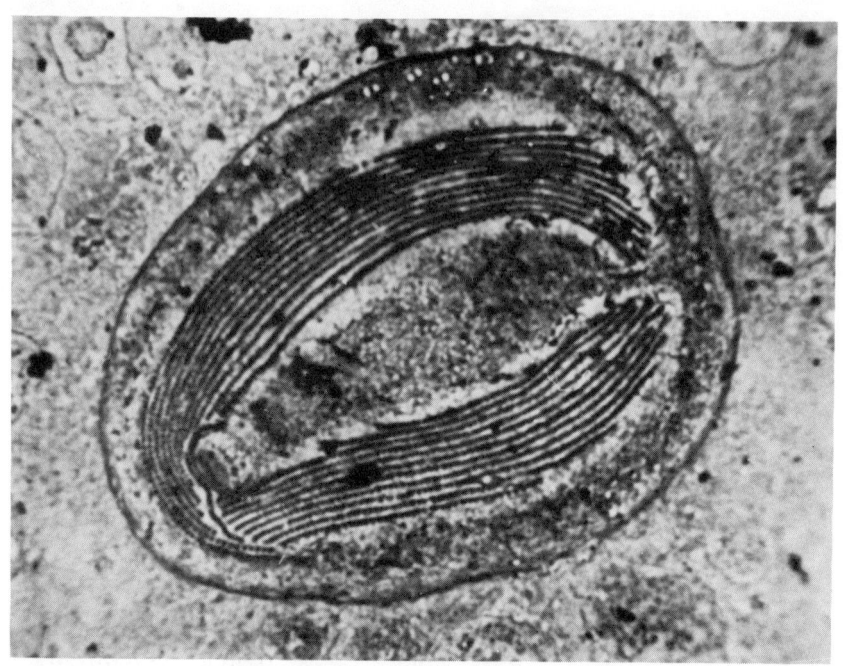
Chilodonella infestation can be fatal to the fish. Photo by Dr. Lom.

damaged, we could also transfer the fish to a special tank. The tank has to be left empty for some time afterwards, but even then we cannot exclude the possibility of a relapse. We have a wide range of drugs to choose from for the control of skin parasites. For a long-duration bath, acriflavin at 5-10 ppm (5-10 mg per liter of water) or quinine hydrochloride at 10-15 ppm applied over a period of two to three days can be recommended. A very reliable, though somewhat drastic, remedy for these diseases is the application of copper sulfate. One gram is dissolved in one liter of water, and of this standard solution we use one ml per liter of aquarium water. Part of the copper is precipitated as copper carbonate after a few hours and is then no longer fully effective. However, the effectiveness also depends very much on the amount of organic matter in the water, and it is therefore very difficult to maintain an exact concentration over a longer period. For this reason, it is advisable to add a booster dose of 50% after one or two days. The fish react with a black coloration and listless swimming. Treatment should never be carried out after feeding when the fish still have a full stomach.

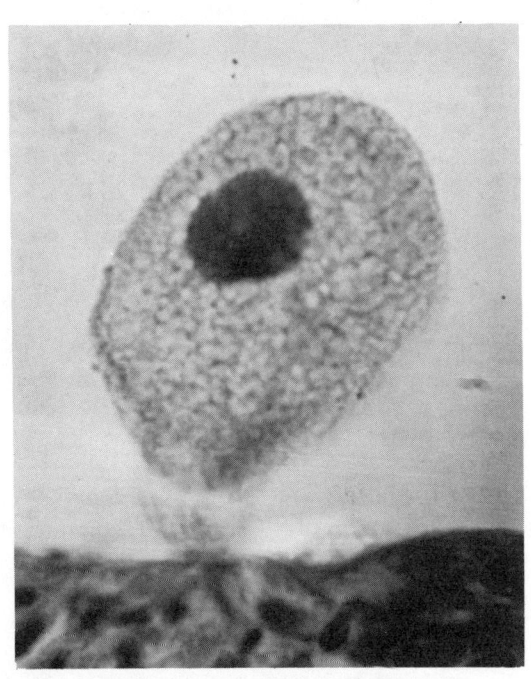

An individual *Oodinium* cell attached to the skin of a fish. Photo by Dr. Robert Goldstein.

A highly magnified photo of *Trichodina*. Photo by Dr. Lom.

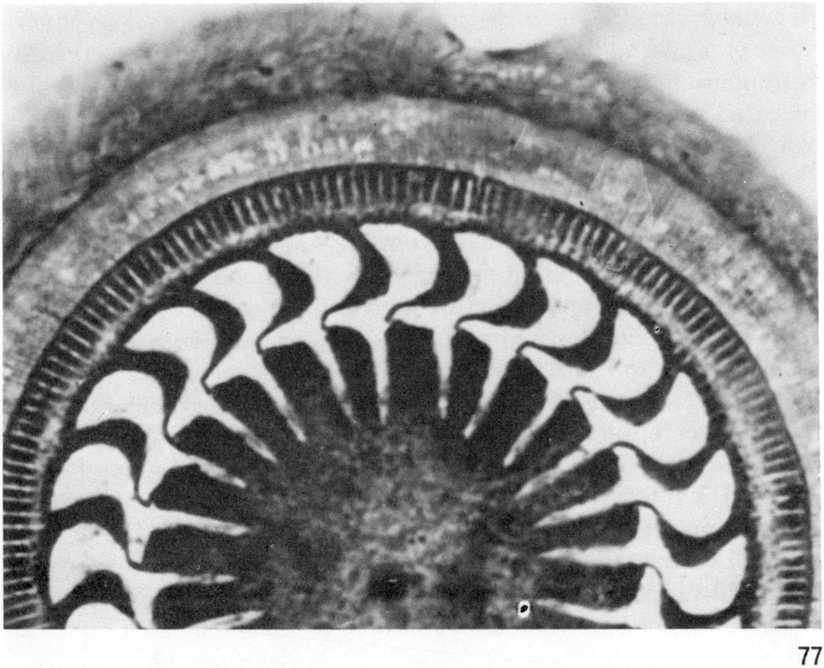

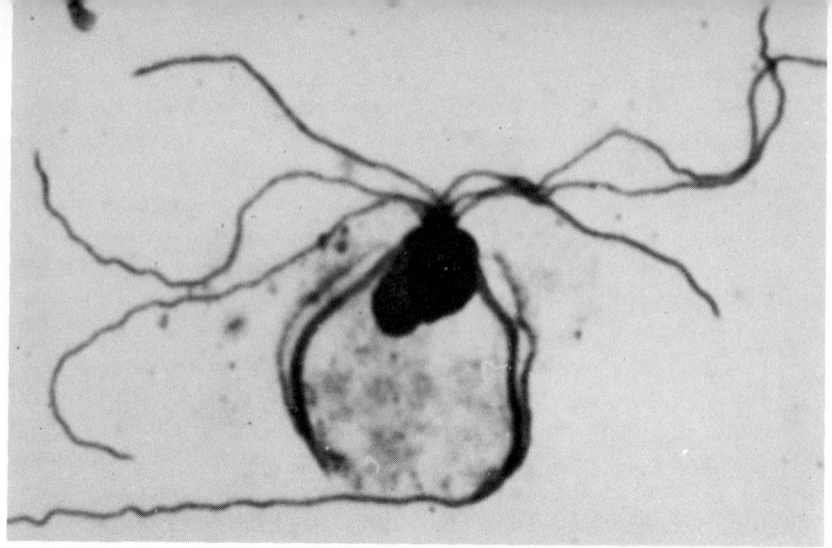

All the flagella (eight) of *Spironucleus* are visible in this photograph. These are locomotory organs characteristic of flagellates or whip-bearing animals. Photo by Dr. Lom.

SPIRONUCLEUS

Spironucleus is another protozoan that gives much trouble to the discus. This parasite, also known under the name *Hexamita*, is a flagellate which lives in the intestine of discus but can also invade other organs, and these are destroyed by it. This unicellular organism is responsible for the early death of many discus. *Spironucleus* was detected a long time ago, but successful treatment has been possible only recently. The worst aspect of an infection with these flagellates is that in the early stages the fish show absolutely no reaction. They feed and swim normally, and their behavior and coloration remain unchanged. Then, one day, they grow fussy about what they eat, and soon they refuse to eat altogether. Now their feces look thin, slimy, and white and the animals grow increasingly apathetic. By the time these obvious signs have appeared the disease has reached a very advanced stage and it is almost too late. The flagellates in the gut—often present in the millions—have severely damaged the organ and, via the circulation, are likely to have spread to the gall-bladder and kidney as well. Then the kidney is no longer able to function properly. That a fish so severely affected as this is often past help hardly need be pointed out.

An early diagnosis is possible only if we examine a specimen of feces. This has to be fresh and should preferably be caught before it reaches the bottom of the tank and then be taken out with a pipette.

Under the microscope, at a magnification of 100 to 200 x, the wriggling flagellates can be seen. Better still, of course, is prevention. Experience has shown that it is virtually impossible to obtain discus which do not harbor these parasites. In addition, the constant danger of infection with flagellates excreted in the feces is particularly great in the aquarium. Good, though temporary, success has been achieved by raising of the temperature, i.e. the aquarium is kept at 37° C. for two to three days. That we require a good thermostat and need to check the temperature at frequent intervals is self-evident. A clinical thermometer is ideal for the purpose. Equally important is good aeration. Many a fish has been saved in this way and was freed of other parasites at the same time. But the possibility of a relapse must never be excluded. Better results are achieved by means of chemotherapy, using commercial remedies specifically formulated to combat *Spironucleus*. Enheptin, Cyzine, carbarsone oxide, and dimetridazole have been used with varying degrees of success. Healthy fish suffer no adverse effects if they are chemically treated every three to six months. But caution is advisable: even here relapses have occurred, presumably because of resistant strains. Certain drugs used in human medicine in the control of *Trichomonas vaginalis*, a flagellate which parasitizes the human reproductive passages, give good results but are available only on prescription.

THREADWORMS

Threadworms of the genus *Capillaria* pose as big a threat to the life of our discus as *Spironucleus*. These worms are very thin, 1-2 cm long and, like *Spironucleus*, live in the intestine of the fish. Again, the only way to find out whether threadworms are present is to examine the feces. The worms lay many eggs, and these eggs are constantly discharged with the feces. The small oval structures look as though they had been sealed with champagne corks at either end.

Frequently, the behavior of the fish indicates that they are infested with worms. If the discus stand perfectly still in the aquarium, barely swimming and eating, with a conspicuous tendency to stand facing the back wall, and their bellies look slightly distended, they are almost certainly suffering from *Capillaria* infestation. The feces may be thin and white, like those observed in *Spironucleus* infections, as the worms fix themselves to the intestinal wall and destroy it. One gets the impression that the fish is expelling its destroyed intestine. Where there is a secondary infection with *Spironucleus*, as not infrequently happens, things do not look too good for the discus. Fortunately there is now a drug, Dylox, developed not so long ago, which

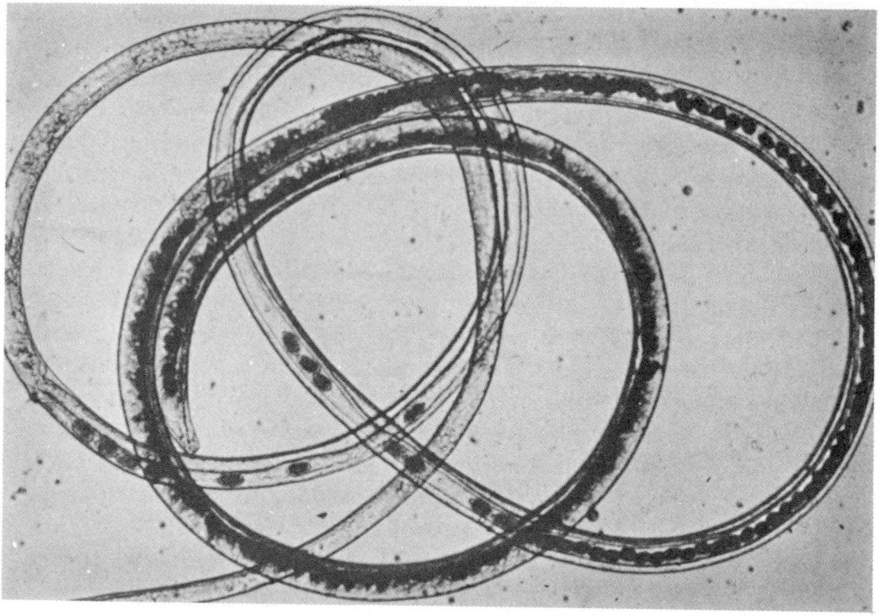

The bead-like structures along the body of this *Capillaria* worm are eggs. Not needing an intermediate host in its life cycle, *Capillaria* can infect all the fishes in a tank. Photo by Frickhinger.

Highly magnified eggs of *Capillaria,* a threadworm. Photo by Dr. Gottfried Schubert.

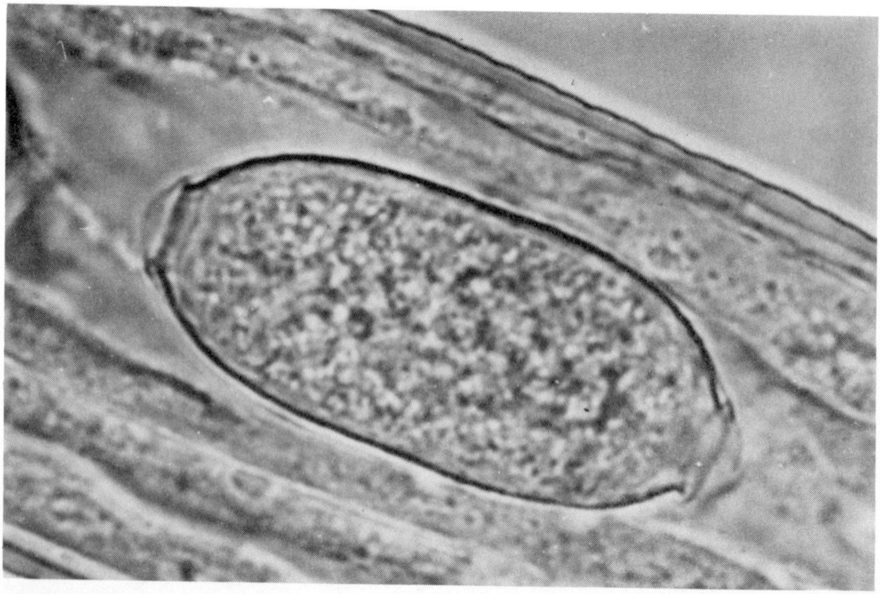

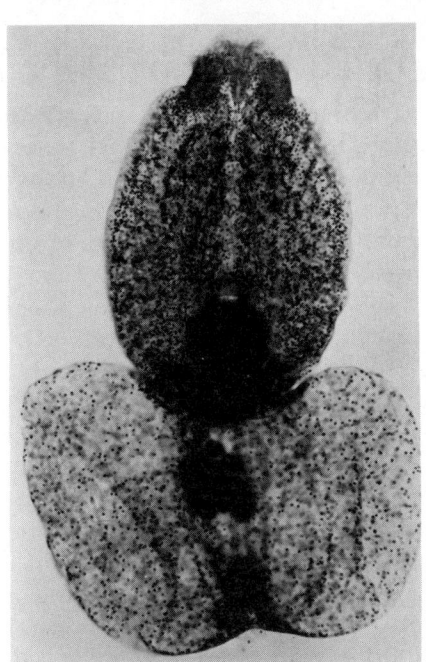

This larval monogenetic fluke was taken from an imported discus. Discus bred in captivity do not harbor this type of parasite. Photo by Dr. Gottfried Schubert.

does much to combat these worms; it was developed for the control of skin and gill worms in pond fishes. This drug is equally suitable for aquarium fishes and brings excellent results. Experience has shown that it is also effective in the control of threadworms. One has to be careful to administer the right dosage, however. If 4 mg per 1 liter aquarium water are given, all *Capillaria* inside the fish will be killed. This dose is ten times as high, however, as recommended for gill worms. Discus tolerate this, but other fishes—such as the neon tetra—quickly die. During treatment, the water temperature should not be above 28° C. After three days it is necessary to change the water and filter it over charcoal. Again, it is better by far to prevent the infestation in the first place, and there is one effective way of doing so. Live bloodworms are able to store many of the substances which are dissolved in the water, so we put a minute quantity of this drug into a dish containing live bloodworms and the larvae absorb a great deal of it before they themselves come to grief. A food treated in this way carries the drug straight into the body of the fish and kills off the parasites. If we supply this food in small amounts, there is no risk of an overdose. The advantage of this method lies in the fact that the drug goes straight to the focus of the disease; the water is hardly affected at all, which means a change of water and specific filtration are not required.

WORMS PARASITIZING THE SKIN AND GILLS

Unfortunately our discus are not spared by these parasites either. These flukes are represented by several genera and species and are commonly regarded as "debility parasites"—they don't kill, they just weaken. However, if the parasites multiply greatly and rapidly, they can also be the primary cause of disease and a fish can die if its gills have been severely attacked. The fry are particularly at risk owing to conditions in the rearing tank. Contact with other fishes, notably in tanks in pet shops, always carries a risk of infection. Mild infestation is usually tolerated without any kind of reaction. When the worms have become a nuisance the fish start to scratch themselves on solid objects, particularly when the skin is affected too. Severe infestation of the gills results in an abnormally fast respiration. An exact diagnosis can be made only with the aid of a microscope. To be absolutely certain, we would have to sacrifice an animal and examine each individual gill filament. But what aquarist would want to do that? Experts take a smear from a living or anaesthetized animal. Dr. Schubert has commented on this in detail. Then we can see whether gill-parasitic worms are present, and their structure tells us what genus they belong to. Those with four black spots at the anterior end (= eyes) are dactylogryrids. They are found mainly on the gills and lay eggs. If the head has two points and there are no eyes to be seen, we are confronted with *Gyrodactylus*. The latter are livebearers and therefore easier to combat. All have a hook apparatus by means of which they attach themselves to the epidermis and, above all, to the gill tissue. Here they literally tear out bits of tissue. Severely affected fish are visibly inhibited in their growth.

Again we are very fortunate to know of the drug Dylox. A concentration of 0.4 ppm (.4 mg per liter of water) is sufficient. These small amounts have to be weighed on apothecaries' scales, however. The subsequent procedure is the same as in the treatment of *Capillaria*. Because *Dactylogyrus* lays eggs, a once-only treatment would achieve very little. It should be repeated at least once, a week later. It should be mentioned, in this context, that the drug causes a slight decoloration of the fish. The beautiful blue changes to silver-green, and the color of the body grows lighter. Another side effect is a somewhat poor appetite. However, since the drug brings good results, is tolerated at the concentration I mentioned, and the fish do not have to be transferred to another tank, it is definitely to be preferred to any other method of treatment. The short baths in sodium chloride or formalin, as recommended in the past, have thereby become superfluous.

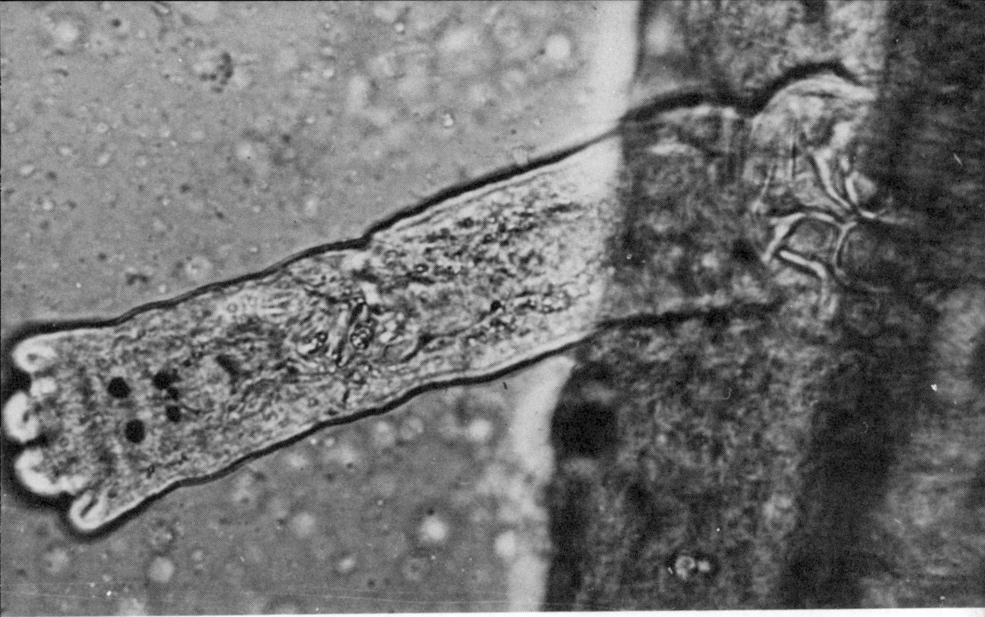

Dactylogyrus attached to the gill tissue of a fish. The four lobes and eye-spots are characteristic of this fluke. Photo by Dr. Gottfried Schubert.

Gyrodactylus also attacks the gills, but this fluke lacks the eye-spots and has only two lobes. Photo by Dr. Gottfried Schubert.

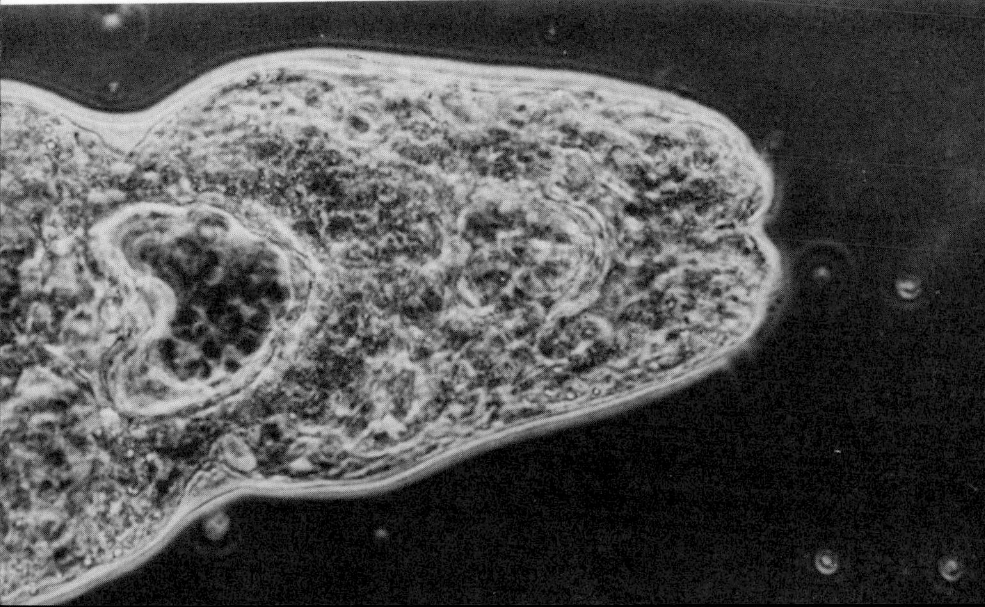

"HOLE DISEASE"

Although the majority of discus keepers have already made the acquaintance of this disease, scientists are still not able to tell us its exact causes. The main characteristic of this disease is the growth of a small white worm-like substance in the skin, usually in the head region, particularly on the forehead and above the eyes. This phenomenon might almost be said to resemble a prominent "blackhead." This growth goes away and leaves a relatively large hole behind. If the water is very clean—i.e., containing few bacteria—and the fish look healthy and strong, the hole quickly closes up again and soon ceases to be visible. But if we are less lucky, the hole grows septic and may develop into a large festering sore. Such animals are in acute danger and must be treated. Treatment is aimed mainly at the infection. Very effective in this respect is Rivanol. One tablet (100 mg) is dissolved in 100 ml water; with this solution one dabs the affected areas on the fish after taking the animal out of the water. In most cases the wound heals. Good results are also achieved with antibiotics such as Terramycin (4 capsules to 100 liters water) or sulfanilamide which are mixed into the aquarium water. The suggestion that *Hexamita* is the causative agent of the hole disease must be doubted, since the hole disease also occurs in animals which have been treated for and are free from *Hexamita*. Furthermore, fish suffering from the hole disease usually continue to have a good appetite. In the same way, there are incidents of animals free from tuberculosis which get these holes. So there is still a lot that needs to be found out. At the first signs of the hole disease it is advisable to change the diet and provide food which is particularly rich in vitamins. This can be done by enriching normal food with commerical aquarium vitamin preparations. At the same time we should ensure that the water in the tank is fresh and biologically perfect. In this way we can usually stop the hole disease and for years continue to keep discus without a recurrence of the disease.

FIN ROT

Occasionally, discus show a reduction of the outer edges of the anal and dorsal fins, and the fins become frayed. These fish are almost certainly suffering from bacterial fin rot. Since the fish show no signs of discomfort, it often takes the keeper some time to notice their condition. When we observe the above phenomena we should examine the aquarium water; fin rot is especially common in old water. The disease responds to sulfanilamide, and in most cases the fins grow back to normal.

An extreme case of bacterial fin rot in an African cichlid (*Haplochromis burtoni*). Fin rot can affect discus, too, but is not likely to occur in fish kept in a well managed tank. Photo by Ruda Zukal.

TUBERCULOSIS

This disease also affects discus. The bacilli attack many different organs and can destroy them. In the past, many diseased fishes were thought to be suffering from an *Ichthyophonus* infection, but today we know that in almost all of those cases the diagnosis should have been that of tuberculosis. Effective treatment of the disease is still not known. Constant high temperatures in the aquarium are thought to favor the spread of tuberculosis. The best way to prevent an outbreak of the disease is to create optimal conditions in the aquarium by changing the water frequently and making sure that the fish receive a varied diet.

CONSTIPATION

Constipation is not uncommon in discus. Frequently it indicates that the fish are suffering from a disease of the stomach or intestine. Overfeeding can also result in constipation; very young and "adolescent" discus especially tend to stuff themselves until they threaten to burst. In fact, nutrition lies at the center of the whole problem. It is vital that the fish be given a correct and varied diet. If we give them a monotonous fare consisting mainly of live foods from dirty waters (e.g. bloodworms and *Tubifex*), the danger of inflammation and constipation is particularly great. Constipation can be recognized by a suddenly swollen belly hours after feeding. Usually the fish continue to feed, but there is no elimination of feces. Treatment is not always successful. Sometimes things get back to normal within a day or two, but if the symptoms (distended abdomen, absence of feces) can still be seen after two or three days, we have to take action. Good results can be achieved with salt baths. The salt required for this treatment is the non-iodized type that can be purchased at pet shops. We can leave the fish in the bath for some time. Some aquarists give the advice to remove the constipated fish and briefly "massage" its belly with the fingers, but this is a very dangerous procedure. One might easily apply too much pressure to the abdominal wall, causing internal injuries. If we feed our fish properly and make sure, above all, that their food has a high chitin content, constipation should never occur. Another source of danger is food out of the deep-freeze that has not been properly thawed and is still too cold. It carries a high risk of inflammation.

None of the above information will seem particularly encouraging to the aquarist who is thinking of keeping discus, and some of it may positively frighten him off. Yet we can be thankful for the progress that has been made in recent years. At least we know now what the problems are, and for most of the difficulties that can arise in the care of discus counter measures have already been found. We no longer have to stand back helplessly and watch our discus die a slow death. It would, of course, be beyond the scope of this book to describe all of the diseases that discus can contract, but I have mentioned the conditions that most commonly occur. No doubt other diseases we can at first do nothing about will crop up in the future. But scientists will consider them a challenge, and one should not hesitate to forward diseased animals for examination. Often this proves helpful both to oneself and to other aquarists. The main thing to remember is that if the discus are kept under optimal water conditions and the food they receive is good and varied, they will give us pleasure for a long time and should, on the whole, remain free from disease.

THE HISTORY OF THE DISCUS

It is interesting to look back and see how discus became an aquarium fish. The angelfish (*Pterophyllum scalare*), cousin to the discus, had already found its way into hobbyists' tanks and had been acclaimed the king of freshwater aquaria by the time discus arrived on the aquarium scene. Its appearance and majestic behavior enthralled aquarists of the 1920's and 1930's, and after a while it became possible—notably by artificial rearing—to propagate this fish, which brought the price of the fish down and enabled many aquarists to keep it. But no sooner had the angelfish become established in aquaria than a rumor was heard about the existence of a fabulous blue angelfish. Inquiries by interested breeders and dealers remained fruitless. Nobody had heard anything definite. The Eimeke company in Hamburg was said to have imported the first specimen in 1921, but it did not survive. In 1928 the Berlin wholesalers Scholtze and Potschke tried to import the fish and sent out a collector, but without success. Then in 1932 the Hartel hatchery of Dresden got the opportunity to buy "blue angelfish" in New York. Herbert Hartel, undeterred by the long, tiring and hazardous journey by sea, accepted the offer. His valuable freight, when he returned, included three wild-caught "blue angelfish" for which even then he had already paid the fantastic sum of 1,200 marks—and 1200 marks was a lot of money at that time.

The fish were cared for in the best possible way. Since they were assumed to be a variation of the angelfish, they were kept under the same conditions. But then it was noted that their bodies grew larger than those of angelfish and that their fins had a different structure. In addition, their color was yellowish-brown, only the head and the fins being blue. Worst of all, however—it proved impossible to breed the fish. All attempts to rear and feed the brood artificially failed. The breeding fish were kept under all sorts of conditions, and so was the brood, but always in vain.

However, four years after the Hartels had a stroke of luck. As a spawning substrate they tried out a clay tube. Inside this the fish could spawn undisturbed, and subsequently it would be possible to fish out the tube with the attached eggs. Since the actual process of spawning could not be observed, the breeders had to exercise great patience, but their patience was rewarded. One day two fish came swimming out of the tube, and the body of each fish was covered with fry. The young tore away at the skin and visibly grew bigger. The mystery had been solved. Now the Hartels knew that these were not angelfish, and they also knew why it had not been possible to rear them artificially. The fish concerned were *Symphysodon aequifasciata axelrodi*. The Hartels had achieved a magnificent aquaristic success which did not, however, become widely known. The discus got its first mention in the German literature in a book by J.P. Arnold and Dr. E. Ahl. Here they were named as *Symphysodon discus* Heckel, which later turned out to have been the wrong classification. The discus did not actually become established in German aquaria until after World War II. At that time it was above all the company Tropicarium Frankfurt which, via Holland, imported this fish again. Special credit for the breeding of the discus goes to Dr. Schmidt-Focke. He succeeded in propagating the fish and then published his observations and experiences. After that, other aquarists were also able to report the successful keeping and breeding of the discus.

But while aquarists everywhere were busy with the brown discus, rumors about the blue discus continued to be heard. These fish which had been caught occasionally—and perhaps also had been imported into the United States occasionally—seemed to have made a lasting impression. Interested aquarists kept speculating about them, until one day what many had dismissed as mere gossip became reality. Harald Schultz, the Brazilian ethnologist, had re-discovered the blue discus. His report on the "hunt for the blue discus" fascinated many aquarists at the time. It must have been in 1955 that Harald Schultz saw a harpooned blue discus at the Lago Jurity. He was greatly impressed by its brilliant colors. Presumably he too had previously seen only the brown discus. He wrote that even after its death the fish continued to have splendid shining colors. He noted that the predominant color was an emerald green and immediately suggested that the fish should be called "green discus." It is possible that the specimen concerned belonged to the variety that today would be classified as *Symphysodon aequifasciata aequifasciata*, the green or turquoise discus.

In any event, he determined to collect some of these magnificent discus, but a few years elapsed before he was able to organize a small expedition and return to this area in which he first saw the fish. He got there in December, 1958, when it was almost too late to catch fish in this region. The rain had already caused the lake to swell, and part of the rain forest had been flooded too. A variety of fishes, and the discus in particular, leave such lakes at times like this and move up the brooks into the rain forest. At first by boat and then on foot the march through the dark jungle began, and after several hours the destination was reached. A small brook with overgrown banks was chosen as a likely discus habitat. The beaters set off and with poles and sticks plowed through the water surface and, above all, the bushes and roots on the banks. By this method the fish were driven out of their hiding places and hurried away from the noise. In a suitable place, Harald and his assistants were waiting, ready to throw their nets. They succeeded in catching some of the fish that swam past, all of them of extreme beauty. Then, when they spread nets across the brook, the results got even better. All in all, they caught 86 splendid blue-green discus. But now the real difficulties began. They had only five oil barrels in which to transport the fish, which had to be taken the long way back out of the jungle squeezed into these containers. Heavy rain showers turned the walk into an ordeal, and much water was spilled out of the barrels on the way as the men climbed over fallen trees. By the time the fishermen had their first break, half of the fish had died. The rest were stored inside the nets in a brook. The men were beginning to feel very hungry, and they ate the dead and dying discus. Roasted in the fire, they were said to have been very tasty. Later, when this became known, many aquarists were shocked and annoyed: dream fish which many longed to have a look at, even just once, and for which others would have given a fortune, had simply been eaten. But what should the men have done? It seemed a sensible solution. By the following morning only 35 fish were still alive. The rest were eaten for breakfast. When the expedition reached the boats the number of survivors had shrunk to 25. With its big waves the lake had meanwhile become impassable for the light boats, and during this enforced break another 15 discus died. A day later, when the men had reached their destination and, after more delay, the plane arrived, only two of those beautiful green discus reached civilization. Now the discus fever really began to spread, and Harald Schultz was implored by people from America and Europe to go back and get more.

In Germany, Dr. Schmidt-Focke was fortunate enough to be given blue discus by Harald Schultz, and he succeeded in getting them to spawn. The chances looked anything but good. He had received only three specimens, one of which later turned out to be *Sym-*

physodon discus Heckel. To get a pair out of two fish—and better yet, to have that pair turn out to be compatible—was a great piece of luck, but that's how it happened.

Dr. Schmidt-Focke applied all his ambition and all his experience to the task of breeding these singular fish and making them generally available. In the meantime the most important prerequisites for the keeping of the fish had been found out, so they were offered optimal conditions. The tank the blue discus were accommodated in had a capacity of 700 liters. No trouble was spared; soft water was specially collected and changed very frequently. The interior of the tank was kept scrupulously clean and protected the fish from infection of any kind. At the same time the animals were pampered with live food whenever possible. All of the trouble taken did not go unrewarded; after three months the fish began to spawn. However, the eggs fungused. Apparently the male had been unable to fertilize them. A period of waiting and hoping followed, and another three months went by before the first modest number of offspring appeared. Certainly the twenty fry obtained were not many, but the spell had been broken.

A few experienced breeders were now able to prove their expertise with the blue discus. Unfortunately, there still was very little known about the many diseases, and further successes were not achieved. Meanwhile, though, the exporters had heard about the discus too, and Willi Schwartz from Manaus was able to export blue discus to Europe. After the blue discus, some of which had only a few blue lines, came the "royal blue," the new kings. From about 1965 onward, discus of all colors have been imported regularly, and today they are among the standard stock of every big wholesaler.

Willi Schwartz of Manus, Brazil, one of South America's foremost exporters of tropical fishes and a specialist in discus varieties. Photo by Dr. Herbert R. Axelrod.

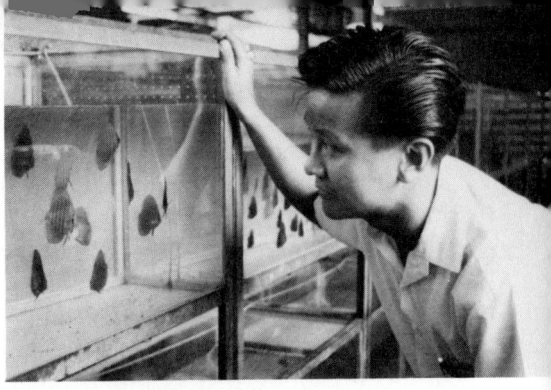

Mr. Virachai of Chao Phraya Aquarium in Bangkok, Thailand, one of the most important raisers of discus in the orient

DISCUS BREEDING IN SOUTHEAST ASIA

That young discus have for some years now been offered for sale at least occasionally at most tropical fish stores is due to a number of enterprising breeders from Southeast Asia. In fact, exporters from that part of the world have for a long time been satisfying most of the demand for many different species of tropical fish on the world market. When discus breeding in the rest of the world was still in many ways dependent on luck, large quantities of cheap little discus were suddenly put up for sale in Southeast Asia. Everybody was baffled and looked for explanations. The discus hatcheries in Asia are centered in Bangkok, Hong Kong, and the Malayan peninsula, especially Singapore. These hatcheries are extremely productive, but there are many small breeders as well who are out to make a good profit on the side.

Why is it that discus breeding is so successful in these areas? The reasons are the same as those responsible for Oriental successes with other species of tropicals. Geologically and climatically these areas offer ideal conditions for the breeding of ornamental fishes. Almost everywhere one finds clean, soft water. It has a total hardness of around 2 German degrees and is very slightly acid—which means it is very similar to the native waters of tropical fishes from South America. Equally ideal is the climate. The temperatures lie within the range of 23-31° C. (average about 27° C.). The breeders exploit these favorable conditions by setting up their hatcheries mostly outdoors. As a rule, the enclosures are covered with simple corrugated iron or canvas roofs. Thus the whole hatchery is in the open air and merely fenced in. The size varies, of course, but generally speaking a hatchery comprises 200 to 300 tanks with a minimum capacity of 100 liters. This means that a lot of work is involved, but laborers are easy to get in Asia, and cheap. Such hatcheries are, of course, run without any technological aid, since thermostats, lights, aeration, and filtration are not required. Every day one-third of the water in each tank is simply allowed to run out and is replaced with fresh water. These are ideal conditions, very similar to natural running waters. The available food is another reason why breeding is so successful here. The food is not only very varied but biologically perfect as well. It is interesting to note that the composition of the "menu" varies a great deal from one country to another. In Thailand, *Culex* larvae (black mosquito larvae) are very common. They are even offered for sale on the market and constitute the staple diet of the blue discus there. It has been reported that the water surface of discus breeding tanks is always partially covered with this food and the fish are, therefore, literally "standing in food." We are familiar with the high nutritional value of these insect larvae, and it was thought by some people that it was this food which lay behind the great success of the Siamese breeders. But the breeders from Malaya and Singapore prove that this is not so. In these countries it is prohibited by law to trade in or breed black mosquito larvae, and the penalty for offenders is very high. Mosquitoes are, of course, the vectors of malaria, and in these countries much has been done to stamp out this disease. That is why this food is taboo here. But the discus breeders can manage without it, because in Malaya and Singapore they have access to large quantities of newly-caught tubificid worms (a very small red species in this locality), and that is what the discus get fed in that area. Usually one can see a small dish of these worms in each tank. Kept in this way, the discus spawn and multiply just as well as they do in Bangkok.

The tanks are completely bare: no bottom layer, no plants. The fish deposit their spawn on the walls, as the tanks do not contain any kind of spawning substrate (such as wood, stones, or flowerpots). By our standards, these aquaria should be called "super hygienic." They are not decorative, but they are successful.

Up to 3,000 fry pass through such a hatchery each month. Owing to the constant changing of the water and the absence of contact with other fishes, coupled with optimal nutrition, diseases and losses are extremely rare in such hatcheries. The breeding stock is in very good condition and often of an impressive size. If the descendants produced from such fish in other countries tend to be delicate and diseased at first, the export centers are surely to blame, not the breeders. Very few hatcheries export discus themselves. Most are sold to wholesalers for trans-shipment. Often, however, the discus are too small for travel, and the risk of infection is particularly high when many fish are squeezed into a small space and come into contact with other fishes or equipment as well. Over and above that, there is always a long, exhausting shipment, and this pushes up the losses still more.

Until now discus breeding in Southeast Asia has been merely quantity-oriented. Whatever was willing to mate was cross-bred, and therefore only brown and green discus were available. But the green discus did not have the same color as wild fish and differed considerably from the green discus that came from Peru and Brazil. Due to constant cross-breeding with brown variations, the beautiful green stripes developed into a weak, blurred, uniform green. In the same way, *Symphysodon discus* Heckel was constantly cross-bred with brown and green variations. But neither one species nor the other was improved in their coloration by this procedure. It can be hoped, however, that before long the breeders will adapt their methods to market demands. Then they will become more selective and supply pure blue, turquoise, and green varieties as well.

How commercialized even fish breeding has become can be seen from the artificial coloring of discus which I mentioned earlier. One can only hope that aquarists will reject such fish and thereby get the breeders to change their methods. It would be far more desirable if, instead, the breeders turned their attention to the selection of especially beautiful and strong breeding stock, as this would in time surely result in at least a small percentage of "pure" animals with prominent colors. In the United States and Europe it will never be possible, despite all expertise, to breed discus so cheaply and on such a massive scale. But this should not discourage us, because Asia doesn't have anything near a monopoly on the production of good discus.

Regardless of whether you buy home-grown stock, Asiatic stock, or wild-caught discus straight from South America, let me give you some advice about what to look for and what to avoid. If a small discus has an exceptionally long body in proportion to its height and has in addition what is referred to as a "knife-edge back" (which means that it has a very skinny "neck"), stay away from it; if in addition to the foregoing warning signs it also swims listlessly, avoid it at all costs. Healthy discus look lively and spread their fins. These are the characteristics one should look out for, regardless of the "bargain" that is being offered. Anyone who has never kept discus before would do well to start off with the relatively inexpensive brown discus. Once a hobbyist has gained experience he can go a step further and acquire blue or green discus, which cost a bit more. Or, of course, one could decide to obtain a few wild-caught fish, but they are still very expensive.

THE DISCUS IN THE FUTURE?

The discus has been the center of attention for many aquarists for many years. Acclaimed as "The King," the discus is desired by many hobbyists—it is a fish that has incited ambition and aroused enthusiasm, but it has also been the cause of envy and intrigue. Let us hope it is, at least in the majority of cases, a love of nature that makes aquarists wish to acquire this fish. Owing to limited stocks, discus are more expensive than most other aquarium inhabitants. With the increased import of wild catches and more intensive breeding in captivity, however, this situation could quickly change.

Unlike the neon tetra, for example, the discus is never seen in very large numbers. There is a very real danger that the discus, too, will lose its proud appearance through indiscriminate mass breeding. Its cousin, the angelfish, has gone the same way. Responsible fish breeders, therefore, always do their best and make sure that the natural beauty of these fish is preserved. The hard road of trial and error can be avoided by anyone who reads this book carefully and follows the advice it has given. The methods described here have been tried out by me over a period of 15 years, during which time I have constantly been engaged in the keeping and breeding of discus. It is fascinating and beautiful to take part in a miracle of creation and to observe how this miracle comes to pass. I would advise the reader to try discus for himself—and I hope there has been something in this book that has helped the hobbyist in his efforts to provide the best of care for his aquarium favorites. Then my work has been worthwhile and fulfilled its purpose.

INDEX

All page numbers in *italic* type refer to photographs or illustrations.